FACE
READING

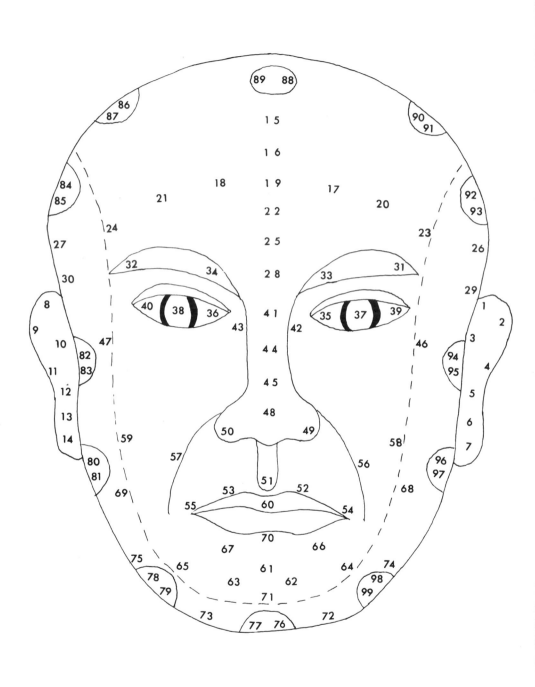

FACE READING

THE CHINESE ART OF PHYSIOGNOMY
BY TIMOTHY T. MAR

DODD, MEAD & COMPANY   NEW YORK

Drawings by Edward J. Klejnowski

ISBN: 0-396-06981-9
Library of Congress Catalog Card Number: 74-6806
Printed in the United States of America

CONTENTS

FOREWORD   vii

1   EAST AND WEST   I
2   "YOUR FACE IS YOUR FORTUNE"   7
3   ZONES AND SHAPES   15
4   THE POSITION SYSTEM   22
5   THE FIVE VITAL FEATURES   30
6   THE EYEBROWS   32
7   THE EYES: GLITTER   37
8   THE EYES: EYE SHAPES, IRISES, AND EYELIDS   41
9   THE NOSE   50
10   THE MOUTH   61
11   THE EARS   69
12   THE FOREHEAD   75
13   THE GROOVE, WRINKLES, CHEEKLINES, MOLES, AND BEARDS   79
14   CHEEKBONES, JAWBONES, CHIN   93
15   LONG LIFE, SHORT LIFE?   98
16   PROBLEMS OF APPLICATION   102
17   PHOTO ANALYSIS   106
18   NOW ANALYZE YOURSELF!   150

FOREWORD

CHINESE chronicles abound with stories concerning physiognomy—the art of face reading. Permit me to cite two examples to show the importance the Chinese attach to it.

Liu Pang, a village constable, met one day with Master Lu, an expert physiognomist. The latter took one look at the constable and immediately offered his daughter in marriage. Within a few years the petty village official established himself as the first emperor of the Han Dynasty (206 B.C.–A.D. 219).

Then there is the case of Chen Po, a famed face reader and friend of General Chao Kuan-yin. The physiognomist recognized and forecast a royal destiny for the general, and in less than a decade the general emerged as the first emperor of the Sung Dynasty (960–1276).

Traditionally, most Chinese are familiar with face reading and practice it to some degree. A few become experts and acquire almost mystical insight into a person's fate and personality. To the expert physiognomist, every face is a map of the past, present, and future. That the expert can read the map with uncanny accuracy has been demonstrated repeatedly through the centuries.

This book is the first attempt to reveal the secrets of Chinese physiognomy to the Western world. I have written in plain language to permit the layman to understand physiognomy's general principles and, more importantly, its practical application. It opens a new door of knowledge to the Western world.

Special features in some of the chapters are particularly important. The principle of balance and proportion is paramount in face reading because it provides clues to a person's general character and fate. The Position System is the key to the practical application of the Five Vital Features: eyebrows, eyes, nose, mouth and ears. These Five Vital Features focus on the relationship between facial features and personality traits and destiny. Other facial features, such as forehead, cheekbones, jawbones, chin, and groove (beneath the nose tip), are also integral parts of the face-reading system. Finally, this book contains a number of case studies and analyses of prominent personalities to incorporate what the student has learned in preceding chapters.

Chinese physiognomy is an integrated system, since facial features are closely interrelated to one another. Accuracy in reading depends entirely on the expertise of the reader in weighing all factors according to their respective and interrelated values.

While the complete system of face reading may appear complex at first, a careful study of each chapter will show that, taken step by step, it is simple to learn and easily applicable to everyday life. With practice, you can develop expertise in reading faces. There is, of course, no substitute for experience. In face reading the subjects are everywhere, in every context—on television, in magazines and newspapers, on the bus or subway, at a party, and so forth. A growing expertise will add a new dimension to your life through analysis of yourself as well as others.

In the present work I have drawn on the following basic material: *Ma Yi Physiognomy* by Chen Po, written in the tenth century; *Liew Chuang Psysiognomy* by Yuan Liew-chuang, published in the fourteenth century; *Tieh Kwan Dao* by Yun Ku Shan Jen, written in the fifteenth century; and *Shui Chin Chi* by Fan Wen-yuan, published in the seventeenth century. These four works constitute the hard core of the Chinese study of physiognomy and are still widely used in contemporary China.

In addition, I have consulted old classics such as the *Bamboo Chronicles* of the third century and Ssuma Chien's *Historical Annals* of the first century B.C. Other works consulted include *Yen Shan Sacred Book of Physiognomy*; the popular edition of the *Complete Physiognomy*, collected and published by Pei-Yi Publishing Company, Taiwan; and a large number of contemporary studies in Chinese and Japanese.

Since 1929 I have known the benefits of several masters of physiognomy. The most outstanding was the late Master Wang Fa-shan, a Taoist scholar who occasionally dropped in at our house in Kuling, a popular summer resort in Central China, to chat with my late father. It was Master Wang who first introduced me to a serious and systematic study of the secrets of physiognomy in the years 1929 to 1934. My memories of this spiritual and scholarly man are long cherished, and it is to him I owe the inspiration for this book.

TIMOTHY T. MAR
Silver Spring, Maryland
1974

CHAPTER 1

EAST AND WEST

SINCE the time of Marco Polo, the Western world has been fascinated by China and things Chinese. The West has even been compelled to invent a word for this form of capitivation—*chinoiserie*. In the twelfth century, when the Polo brothers returned from Cathay, as China was then called, they astonished the West with their reports of gunpowder, printing, and spaghetti (noodles). In our time the reopening and rediscovery of China has once again electrified the West. The rage today ranges from pandas to acupuncture.

But through the centuries, the Chinese art, if not science, of physiognomy has remained where it has lain since it was first developed—beyond the Western horizon. The subject is rarely, if ever, discussed, and most Westerners do not even know that the Chinese have excelled in the development of physiognomy—that is, the revelation of an individual's personality and probable fate by a study of his or her face.

This ignorance in the West is astonishing and doubly perplexing to me. In the first place, the West's closed mind on the subject defies the history of Western civilization. As Robert Maynard Hutchins, the former president of the University of Chicago, has observed, "The spirit of Western civilization is the spirit of inquiry." In the West, he points out, this spirit means that nothing under the sun is to remain undiscussed and unexamined. In effect, everybody is to speak his mind, and through the exchange of ideas Western civilization is to continue its forward thrust.

In the second place, the idea that there is a relationship between your facial features and your personality and fate is hardly new to Western thinking. For example, in about 340 B.C. Aristotle wrote eloquently on the subject as he set out along the path pioneered by Hippocrates. "When men have large foreheads," he observed in his *History of Animals*, "they are slow to move; when they have broad ones, they are apt to be distraught; when they have foreheads rounded or bulging out, they are quick-tempered." Aristotle, whose powers of analytical reasoning were perhaps his greatest contribution to the Western world, then proceeded to analyze the salient features of the human face. Straight eyebrows, he informs us, are a sign of softness of disposition. Harshness of disposition is suggested by eyebrows that curve toward the nose. If the eyebrows are drawn toward one another, jealousy may be a dominant personality trait. And so on.

Those of us living in the Western world need not be familiar with the writings of Aristotle to realize that we pepper our language with physiognomic phrases, although not necessarily aware of what we are doing: "He has an honest face"; "I don't like the look of her eyes"; "He has a sinister cast." There are countless other illustrations; think about it the next time you make such a remark.

Winston Churchill, for example, had a bulldog jaw, and it was universally felt among Westerners of all political dispositions that he also had a bulldog's tenacity, which he did. This is a vivid illustration of how a facial feature may reveal a personality trait.

When American Airlines recently launched a multimillion-dollar publicity campaign, it lured Chet Huntley, the former news commentator, from retirement to deliver the advertising message on television because "his face can sell anything." And lately, in a move to check the rise in sky piracy, U.S. air marshals have developed a "hijacker's profile" for spot-checking passengers at airports. Without realizing it, both the airline and the government are using face reading as a practical tool.

I should hasten to add that the idea that the face may reveal a person's character is not limited to Asia and the West. South of the Sahara, in Black Africa, a Congolese chieftain in ancient times kept his face completely covered from the couriers of other tribes. Only his eyes were visible. This has never been satisfactorily explained in the West. Sir James Frazier, in his monumental book *The Golden Bough*, suggests the chieftain was trying to ward off evil spirits. Perhaps. But in the light of Chinese face-reading experience, it may well be that he was anxious not to reveal his character to the courier of a potential rival or adversary.

The same may be said of the monarchs of medieval Europe. In the age of kings, summitry was frowned upon for fear that the personalities of opposing monarchs might clash or that a monarch might reveal his character to another—a valuable piece of intelligence. Indeed, in our modern era some politicians frown on summitry for similar reasons.

But today we live in an age not of kings but of image-making machines—cameras, photo-copying devices, television, and so forth. The facial appearance of the leaders of the Greater and Lesser Powers are known to all.

In this connection, let me stress at the outset that the diffcrent facial characteristics which distinguish one race from another—an Oriental from an Occidental, for example—are of no consequence in face reading. Chinese physiognomy is primarily concerned with whether a person's eyes are set in their "right places," that is, are in balance and proportion. The face reader does not care whether the sitter's eyes are round or almond-shaped. Thus the secrets of Chinese face reading may be applied universally, irrespective of race, color, and ethnic background.

Wherever you go in the world, the average person accepts the face as primary evidence of identity. Nobody is likely to dispute this observation. Even an unknown skull, British criminologist Nigel Moreland points out, can reveal the victim's race and ethnic background. Why not, he asks, a fleshed-out skull?

Indeed, the more you consider the relationship between

face and personality, the more it is clear that all of us—irrespective of race, religion, or color—are what I call "instant physiognomists."

When you meet a person for the first time, you make an instant, intuitive judgment. You may or may not correct or modify that view later on. Nevertheless, the point is that on the basis of a person's facial appearance you are apt to judge character.

As compared to China, however, more often than not such judgments in the West are made haphazardly. Only the Chinese, over the course of centuries, have developed a scientific literature that trains a person to avoid pitfalls in making a personality judgment on the basis of a person's facial features.

In the West the prejudice against physiognomy, as in the case of acupuncture, runs deep. The *Encyclopaedia Britannica* is a spectacular case in point. It treats physiognomy as a "pseudoscience dealing with personality traits supposedly revealed by facial features." If it is a "pseudoscience," why rub salt in the wound by repeating that it "supposedly" links facial features to personality traits? A Freudian slip, perhaps.

Worse, the section on physiognomy was written by Donald G. Paterson, a professor at the University of Minnesota, who dismisses physiognomy as a science and has written several studies to dispute its content. Paterson is hardly a disinterested writer.

Even so, Paterson is forced to concede that since World War II the subject is in "suspended judgment" as a result of the work of W. H. Sheldon, a Western scientist who has found evidence that there is a definite relationship between physical appearance and temperament. Thus Paterson is compelled to retreat. He hedges. "Eventually science may unlock the secret of human character and personality by the co-disciplinary study of the same individuals by specialists in human genetics, biochemistry and psychology," he concludes.

Paterson gives no hint that a vast body of Chinese literature exists on the subject, a literature that has been unfolding for thousands of years. The same may be said for most, if not all, western writers on the subject. Thus we are back to square one. Why has Western man, from the Polo brothers on, blocked out the Chinese experience of determining a person's temperament and destiny from his facial features?

Some fifty years ago in the United States, a small group on the West Coast sought to popularize physiognomy and invented a new word for it, "personology." They contended, without access to Chinese literature, that your face can reveal your personality. They sought to gain academic acceptance for personology but were rebuffed. By practical experience, however, they found that they could help people by providing them with information they could use today to make a better tomorrow.

But the problem was that the movement's founder, Daniel Whiteside, was unable to prove the validity of face reading on a purely scientific basis (anatomic-biologic-neurologic-endocrinologic). This did not necessarily destroy its usefulness. "But just to say something works doesn't bring it scientific acceptance or get rid of vested-interest hostility," Whiteside lamented.

This, of course, has been the problem of acupuncture. In given situations, acupuncture works. But it cannot yet be explained scientifically and is therefore widely suspected by medical doctors in the West.

The Western attitude notwithstanding, from time immemorial face reading has occupied a significant position in the mainstream of Chinese life. Ancient scholars and thinkers wrote extensively on the subject. Chinese historical annals are replete with the facial descriptions of rulers and others. This interest has continued for centuries. In the process, China has developed a sophisticated and rational system of physiognomy which is at once unique, compelling, and practical.

The Chinese system is based on a body of theories, which will be touched on in the simplest of terms at a later point. Theories aside, the Chinese system is a practical method for reading character and, therefore, the future. Every facial sign is interpreted according to a set of rules. There is no haphazard guesswork. The approach is scientific, although physiognomy is no more an exact science than psychology or sociology.

The everyday application of physiognomic knowledge can be extremely fruitful. In many instances physiognomy is like a double exposure. The salesman can evaluate the prospective purchaser and the purchaser can evaluate the salesman. The head of state can size up a diplomatic emissary and vice versa. The employer can analyze the prospective employee and the employee can analyze the employer. Lovers can analyze each other. In still other instances, physiognomy is like a single-exposure lens. For example, in an election year a constituency can better judge the character of the candidates by studying their faces on television.

But there is far more to Chinese physiognomy. It goes beyond personality traits and character. As an integrated system, it probes a person's destiny.

To the Chinese face reader, destiny refers to the ups and downs during a normal lifetime. The Chinese physiognomist, by studying your face, does not simply conclude that you are going to have success or failure in life and leave it at that. Chinese physiognomy has been refined to the point where the face reader, with extraordinary precision in most instances, can pinpoint the very years of success and/or failure.

Although the Chinese are among the first to emphasize that face reading is not a pure science, they point out that it has stood the test of centuries. Chinese face reading is based on literally millions of test cases.

In this period of renewed interest in China and things Chinese, the time is at hand for the West to peek over the physiognomic horizon. What follows, then, is the first attempt at comprehensively presenting this ancient Chinese system to the West.

CHAPTER 2

"YOUR FACE IS YOUR FORTUNE"

BEFORE plunging directly into the basic subject matter, I must introduce a note of caution to Western readers.

In the Western world physiognomy is defined as an attempt at analyzing a person's character by reading his or her face. In China it is all this and much more.

Since its earliest development, in the epoch before the birth of Christ, physiognomy in China has been treated—like acupuncture—as a branch of medicine. The reasoning is simple. Since a person's facial features reflect his personality or inner vitality, an individual's appearance is closely related to his mien, his spirit, and, therefore, his physical well-being. More than two thousand years later, Western psychiatry confirmed this assessment.

But going beyond this, China's physiognomists have long maintained that the shape and position of facial features and other characteristics will reveal not only a person's character but also his "fate."

If a person's personality can be read from the signs on his face, the Chinese believe, then so can his future. Again, the reasoning is not complicated. Facial features change in the aging process. Each change in a person's features provides a clue to his behavior, to his well-being, and therefore, perhaps, of things to come. The Chinese contend that we need only detect and analyze these changes as they occur, especially skin coloring, to peek into a person's future. In a sense, to use a Western metaphor, "your face is your fortune."

However, the suggestion that we are fated to what we become in life tends to turn off most Western minds. In the West, I know, everyone is supposed to be in control of his destiny. Most Westerner's strongly feel that a person's character, intelligence, ability, resourcefulness, and drive are acquired through education, experience, and discipline. And, in turn, this contributes to shaping his future, to making him or her a success or failure in life.

Perhaps. But Asians also believe that fate is reality. For example, last year a jet fighter plane crashed in a California residential area and killed twenty people. The Chinese called the incident a matter of fate. westerners called it something else. Indeed, most Westerners toy with the notion that they are masters of their fate. When they find they are powerless in a given situation, such as an earthquake, they pray to God. The Chinese see events, whether an airplane crash or an earthquake, not as an accident or act of Divine Providence but as fate, something simply to be accepted. This is a fundamental difference between Occidental and Oriental.

Throughout this book, then, the terms "character" and "fate" should be understood to represent a linkage, as far as face reading is concerned.

Chinese face readers believe that in addition to the constant change in one's facial features, we all possess inborn qualities (not many Westerners would argue against this conclusion). True, a person may be able to muster enough willpower to effect an inner change. But this change or improvement is limited at best, for willpower is limited from birth. Chinese physiognomists believe that each person lives out his life within a basically fixed pattern. This pattern is reflected on his face and it differs from all others, just as the whorls on a person's fingerprints differ.

If no two people are exactly alike in their patterns of fate, then, Chinese face readers contend, the difference between them—their facial features—is a key to the mystery of why.

Thus each person's fate, like his face, has its own individual characteristics. If one face has features of a special type that can be identified with an extraordinary achievement or a colossal failure, for example, this same face type can serve as a guide to others with similar facial features.

This concept is at the heart of Chinese face reading—the ability to learn simple facial patterns and their meaning. But the subject is complicated by innumerable variables.

If the Western mind seems puzzled by the evidence, then think in terms of Oscar Wilde's tale, *Picture of Dorian Gray.* The successive changes in the painting of Gray accurately reflected his fate, his moral decay, and his descent into a living hell, his ultimate fate.

Even so, the Western mind probably rejects the concept of "fate" as unscientific. Of course, as observed earlier, the Chinese do not consider physiognomy an exact science, any more than Westerners consider psychology or sociology a pure science or, for that matter, "political science" a true science.

Physiognomy *cannot* analyze a person's character or forecast his future with mathematical precision. But in the course of literally thousands of years of research, physiognomy has proven amazingly accurate.

The principal reason physiognomy is not a pure science is that much of the success in a physiognomical reading rests on the reader's ability to analyze the variables in a face. This ability varies unevenly among physiognomists just as an interpretation of dreams may vary among psychiatrists.

To understand the basics of how physiognomy works, let us consider some faces.

When we view the face of a world figure, a de Gaulle or a MacArthur, we can readily observe strong features—the eyebrows, eyes, nose, and cheekbones, for example, all in good balance and proportion. When the possessor of such a face looks directly at us, we cannot help feeling a penetrating gaze and charismatic personality. In other words, we feel the force of his inner vitality through his eyes— what the Chinese call "glitter" (a word we shall use often). We can appreciate that this person is a leader in the full sense of the word. Thus, in China it is said that such a person is a born leader because he was born with these features.

Don't scoff at the idea. In the West you frequently hear statements such as: "He is a born loser"; "She was born lucky"; and so forth.

But, you ask, what if a person does not seem to possess powerful features and yet is a powerful leader? Suppose he has an "ordinary" face? How do the Chinese texts explain this?

In such a case there are two possible explanations. The individual may have positive features that are hidden or unintelligible to the person unfamiliar with physiognomy. Or the individual may have risen to leadership as a result of accident or opportunity. In the latter case, his prominence is likely to be short-lived and his career cut short at the summit by disappointment, disgrace, or disaster. The unsuccessful revolutionary is a case in point, and so is a Rasputin or Richard III.

Then there are people such as child stars and child prodigies who reveal their talent at a young age. They have full, high, broad foreheads, long refined eyebrows, large brilliant eyes, and a straight nose—all in perfect balance and proportion with each other. These reflect positive inborn features pointing to early success in life. A continuation of this success into later years can also be predicted if the person's mouth, chin, and ears are in balance and proportion in the upper area of the face.

Leslie Howard is a classic example of this type. As a motion picture star he appeared in such brilliant successes as *Gone with the Wind*, and it is as an actor that he is best remembered by most Americans. But in Europe he is remembered as a designer of the famous Spitfire, the British-built fighter that tilted the scale against the Nazis during the Battle of Britain in 1940. Howard succeeded in his many enterprises because of that rare attribute, a well-balanced and proportioned face.

These examples illustrate the most elementary method of predicting a person's character and future, your own included. The Chinese system of face reading will show how man's personality and man's fate are interwoven.

The Chinese say, with reason, that in the hands of the experienced analyst the rich have never been taken for the poor, the virtuous for the wicked, nor vice versa. What each face reveals is there for the world to see.

BALANCE AND PROPORTION

The first principle of face reading, then, is an understanding of balance and proportion. A nose should be neither too large nor too small when compared to the other features of the face. If it is not in good proportion to other facial features, it is considered in that light.

For example, suppose a man has a broad and high forehead (from the hairline to the eyebrows), strong eyebrows, penetrating eyes, and a long nose with a high bridge. Glancing at him, we would say that these features are in their proper balance and proportion. However, further study may reveal that his upper lip is very thin, or that his chin is weak and receding and his cheeks are bony. The whole lower area of the face sags. A Chinese physiognomist would take this into careful consideration before completing his analysis. The reason is that the upper and middle zones of the subject's face overpower the lower zone, the area between the top of the nose and that of the chin. This requires detailed analysis of the mouth and chin to see if there are any redeeming features to compensate for this weakness. This is the only way to determine the individual's character and future.

Before proceeding further, let me reiterate that these conclusions are based on centuries of recorded observation in China. This is not guesswork or crystal-ball gazing, although that is what a superficial Westerner might conclude.

When a Chinese physiognomist says that a person has a strong face, he means that he has strong features reflecting the strength of his character, his inner personality, inner vitality. His penetrating eyes, straight nose, firm mouth and jaws point in this direction. A closer examination will reveal that the flesh on his face is full but not fat, firm but not rigid. His facial skin as a whole is soft, flexible, and not stretched so tight as to show bones. On the cheeks there are no horizontal lines to indicate the muscle growth against the grain. All these are part of the principle of balance and proportion, because the features alone do not make a good face without having the flesh and skin considered together.

By the same token, the face reader must not hastily draw a conclusion on the evidence of only one facial feature. He can do so only if he analyzes the whole face. The reason is that often one good feature can cancel out a bad one, and one bad feature can compromise a good one. This mirrors the principle of balance and proportion, and it must be carefully applied to ensure accuracy.

Therefore, the more a person's facial features are in balance and proportion, the stronger his character and the better his fate. Ah, you say, what if all the basic features are not in balance or proportion? Should the physiognomist dismiss this face as hopeless? Not at all.

When the face reader is confronted with such a face, he should try to weigh it in an entirely different light. He should seek some kind of unity from these irregular features and thereby form a new standard for judging the face in front of him.

All things are relative; the theory of relativity does not only work in the West. Let us say, for example, an individual's forehead is narrow and low, the eyebrows long and untamed, the eyes small and glitterless, the nose crooked, the chin weak and receding, the ears soft and small—a perfectly "ugly" face to the casual observer. But though every feature is bad and far below the popular standard, there is still a semblance of unity.

Unity, therefore, means that one negative feature matches another negative feature, and all the negative features together result in an innate balance and proportion of its own. Such cases are not rare at all. This is the so-called "ugly" face, a face of an Abraham Lincoln or a Mrs. Eleanor Roosevelt, people of warm character, great humanity, and stunning success.

A Chinese physiognomist would explain that the character and fate of such "ugly" persons reflects their inner vitality, their glitter. As long as a person has a forceful inner vitality, his irregular facial features can display strength if there is unity. And glitter or inner vitality is revealed by the unity of the face. Thus unity or balance and proportion must be taken together as a whole. The term "unity" is a relative one, just as modern psychologists and psychiatrists employ the term "normal": In a madhouse, relatively speaking, madness is "normal."

The Chinese system of face reading requires of the face reader a cultivated mind, a mind that is perceptive, systematic, and analytic. Of course, the same type mind is required of a medical doctor. In physiognomy there are two reasons for this. First, as in the case of the psychiatrist, the face reader must display empathy toward the sitter, since the reading requires that the reader draw on all his vital energy for concentration. Second, the Chinese believe a cultivated person has a greater interest in relating his art to human welfare. But even the casual or cosmetic reader, they feel, fulfills a social need, and this includes fortunetellers, numerologists, and so forth.

Since true face readers in China are cultivated, learned men, they are automatically Confucian moralists. Confucianism, briefly, is the system of ethics propounded by Confucius and his disciples. It is based on the cardinal virtues of filial piety, benevolence, justice, propriety, intelligence, and fidelity. Chinese physiognomists read people's faces within the context of Confucian moral teachings, and therefore they believe that their services will have positive value.

Like any medical doctor in the Western world, a physiognomist is not only steeped in moral teachings but also knows how to make use of them in lending to himself an aura of authority, and even a touch of mysticism. The face reader does so in the conviction that true service to humanity is thus rendered.

Even the itinerant face reader never ceases to lecture, preach, and persuade the sitters that bad luck is the result of one's defiance of Nature, and that the only remedy is to appease one's destiny. In doing this, the face reader brushes aside, of course, an underlying principle of physiognomy— that the fate reflected on a face is immutable.

This is the physiognomist's paradox, and he knows it. Thus the face reader, like a Western physician, mixes his face reading with goodness of heart and a touch of piety, and develops a "bedside manner." The face reader uses discretion so as not to frighten the sitter. If the message is negative, he tries to get it across without blurting it out in so many words. Accordingly, face reading in China is a "gentle art," at once sophisticated and subtle.

The role of the physiognomist is like that of a messenger of contradictory tidings. He points out the inevitability of fate, and he infuses into the sitter a sense of reverence or contrition. The fortunate are cautioned not to be overweaning. The unfortunate are exhorted to improve their lot. All this is in line with the Chinese "Doctrine of the Mean," which aims to harmonize contradictions and keep the conduct of life in balance and proportion with a view to avoiding all forms of extremism and violence.

Yet below the surface, hard-headed logic prevails. Since a person is born with his face, "his face is his fortune." Although modern plastic surgery may alter a person's appearance, it is only skin-deep and can never alter a person's character or fate. In any event, as one noted criminologist recently observed, plastic surgery is "more common to Hollywood B-thrillers than to real life."

Finally, in pursuing the subject of face reading, it is important to repeat, especially in the West, what Chinese physiognomy is not.

Just as it is not a pure science, the Chinese face reader is not a seer in the Western spiritual sense or in the sense of the Hindu fakir. A face reader's analysis does not depend on divination. Nor does he depend on a trance or some sort of Karma to invoke supernatural powers. The Chinese physiognomist views himself as the practitioner of an ancient art form that cannot be wholly scientifically explained, yet has a scientific footing and has been clinically proven to be accurate over the centuries.

CHAPTER 3

ZONES AND SHAPES

ANCIENT CHINESE physiognomists divided the face horizontally into three zones, known as the *San Ting*, namely, the Upper Zone, Middle Zone, and Lower Zone (fig. 1). They also divided the contour of the head into five basic shapes: Oblong, Triangular, Semi-Triangular, Square, and Round (figs. 2, 3, 4, 5, 6). These zones and shapes serve as a key

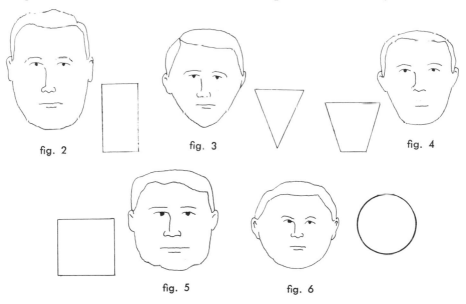

fig. 2   fig. 3   fig. 4

fig. 5   fig. 6

The Position System

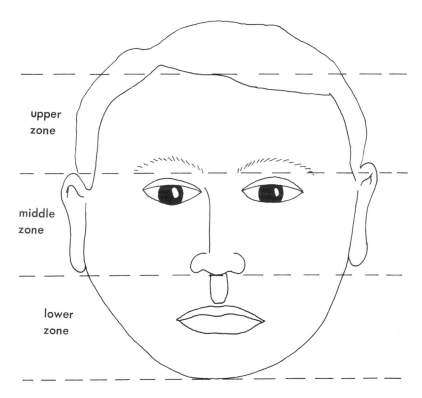

upper
zone

middle
zone

lower
zone

fig. 1

to understanding the secrets of Chinese face reading. Let us therefore analyze each of them.

The Upper Zone (fig. 1) extends from the hairline on the top front forehead to the eyebrows. This zone governs inherited intellectual faculties, thus reflecting family conditions during childhood. It also tells the story of a person's life, especially between the ages of fifteen and thirty and, oddly enough, the ages of eighty-four and ninety-three

(See the Position System, fig. 7). If a person's forehead is well developed, the individual is apt to be bright, resourceful, and endowed with other characteristics that will lead to success in life. The term "well developed" in this instance means in good proportion to other facial features. The ideal forehead is long and high. However, the ideal forehead must be balanced by wide ears. If the forehead is unusually large, perhaps even out of shape, it is an indication that the individual is mentally defective. If the forehead is narrow and ill-shaped, it indicates a person with a difficult personality and facing continuous adversity, such as the loss of parents early in life.

The Middle Zone (fig. 1) extends from the eyebrows to the tip of the nose. This zone governs the prime years of life, from thirty-five to fifty years of age, and also other periods, including one through seven, eight through fourteen, eighty through eighty-three, and ninety-four through ninety-seven. If the Middle Zone is well developed, it reflects an adventurous spirit, a proud and arrogant personality. A small Middle Zone, especially with cramped facial features, is an indication of mediocrity. If the Middle Zone is long, while the Upper and Lower Zones are of similar length, it suggests a person of noble character. A huge nose bridge, with a round, full-tipped nose, usually belongs to a person who has an aptitude for business. A short Middle Zone, meaning one far shorter than the other two zones, is an indication of a relatively short life. If this zone is well shaped without defect, it indicates long life.

The Lower Zone (fig. 1) extends from below the nose tip to the tip of the chin. It governs the years between fifty-one through seventy-seven, seventy-eight through eighty-one, ninety-six through ninety-nine, the late years of our lives. If the rear of the head is well-developed, then the features within this zone—mouth and chin—should be broad and relatively heavy. Such individuals are affectionately inclined. If the Lower Zone is too broad, the individual is probably very passionate. If the zone is too narrow, the person has little interest in family or friends, tends toward introspection, and prefers a lonely existence. If the zone is too long, the person is prone to mishaps, and hence misfortunes. However, if this zone shows strength of bone structure and flesh it is a sign of success and prosperity late in life. A long and narrow Lower Zone, especially accompanied by a pointed chin, generally indicates a "born loser," a failure in life.

The ideal face has these three zones well proportioned and in balance. That is, all the features of the face are in their "right" places, neither too long nor too small and without defects. The concept of the three zones is also applied to the human body as a whole. The head occupies the Upper Zone, the trunk the Middle Zone, and from the waist down to the toes is the Lower Zone.

Thus a perfect face on a deformed or crippled body calls for an integrated analysis. If the face is great and noble, then the body would not make too much difference. Artist Toulouse-Lautrec and President Franklin D. Roosevelt are good examples of this type. Generally, however, a short person with a huge head is considered to have a defective character; similarly, a person with a huge body and a small head. This also applies to persons with a short, ill-proportioned trunk or an unusually long trunk.

The application of face reading to the whole body, however, is of little concern to us. This is only a small branch of the Chinese system. In fact, most Chinese face readers rely on the face alone for a complete reading of personality and destiny because, in theory, the face reveals a person's whole history. And the ideal face, irrespective of racial or ethnic background, reflects the ideal fate and hence the standard of excellence. Remember, an ideal face is essentially a face that is well proportioned and in balance.

As noted at the outset, Chinese physiognomists divided the shape of the head into five basic patterns. On meeting someone for the first time, a thorough recognition of these shapes will provide you with instant insights into the individual's character and destiny.

fig. 2

The Oblong Shape (fig. 2) is rectangular in form. The breadth of the forehead is about the same as that of the jawline. This is the so-called aristocratic shape because most rulers and persons in places of power have a face of this type. This is the face of an intelligent, sensitive, calculating, farsighted person, one who is also judicious and calm. This face belongs to an individual who has organizing talent and the capacity to work with others to reach a desired objective. This type individual is usually a success in life.

The Triangular Shape (fig. 3) has a high, wide forehead, prominent cheekbones, thin nose, deep-set eyes, and a small, pointed chin. The face is considered bony because there is little flesh in the area between the cheekbones and the chin. This type of man or woman tends to be supersensitive and keeps very much to himself or herself. The Triangular Shape is often associated with "brainy" individuals, intellectuals, thinkers, people with high intelligence quotients. This is also the face of the Walter Mitty, the dreamer, the person given to thoughts and speculations. The Triangular Shape is also associated with individuals who are cunning, jealous, and lacking in loyalty or affection. People with this shape of head may find it difficult to get along with others.

fig. 3

On the positive side, such individuals turn to science, philosophy, or the arts. On the negative side, this type evolve into spies, traitors, and unscrupulous businessmen. People whose heads are Triangular may become outcasts of society. They are apt to stage protests and demonstrations and become the fanatical leaders of unpopular causes. Confronted by failure, such individuals withdraw and become recluses.

The Semi-Triangular Shape (fig. 4) shares much in common with the Triangular Shape, although it differs in many important respects. It consists of a wide forehead, but it lacks a pointed chin. A person with such a face is intelligent, sensitive, and artistic, but lacks a fighting spirit. Many women belong to this type. Such women are affectionate and invariably lead happy married lives.

fig. 4

The Square Shape (fig. 5) belongs to a rugged, masculine, bony type of person who usually has a hot temperament. Such a person is a leader, a great fighter. But these individuals are slow thinkers, stubborn but persistent and determined. They are usually direct and frank in business and love affairs. Individuals with a clear-cut Square Face have a tremendous drive for success and make good executives. Should a woman's face be Square Shaped, it indicates

fig. 5

fig. 6

that she is a fierce competitor in any field of endeavor. In a love affair or marriage this type of woman is the dominant sex.

The Round Shape (fig. 6) is associated with the heavyweight individual. If such a person also has a small nose, it is indicative of an easygoing nature. He loves the comforts of life, is a gourmet and a great lover. He is gentle, soft, and peaceful by nature. He is not overly materialistic nor anxious to pursue fame or position. Such people tend to be unambitious. However, if a person of the Round Shape is endowed with relatively prominent cheekbones, penetrating eyes, and a high-bridge nose, he has an entirely different personality. Then he is a fast thinker with an orderly, efficient mind. In this case he is an activist. Such individuals make good military commanders and police officers.

The foregoing three zones and five shapes serve as the basic introduction to the Chinese system of face reading. You will notice how personality and fate appear to intermix in the system. No face, however, will fit exactly into a set pattern. The average face will combine the features of two or more types. For this reason, the physiognomist's essential task is to study and evaluate a face completely before drawing conclusions about an individual's character or destiny, or combination of both.

An experienced Chinese face reader can tell at a glance the zone and shape of the subject. His rule of thumb is to scan the basic features first—forehead, eyebrows, eyes, nose, cheekbones, chin, and ears—and then form an integrated opinion as to whether the features fit into any one of the Standard Patterns. In doing so, the experienced reader also takes into consideration the person's age, his maturity. An individual may belong to one facial pattern in the middle years and to another in the winter of his life.

The Standard Patterns according to the ancient Chinese texts are:

The Noble Face—that of emperors and kings, presidents and prime ministers, dictators and tyrants. Such people hold awesome power over the lives and deaths of others.

The Superior Face—that of people of great renown. Includes leaders of great movements and people who are gifted organizers.

The Resourceful Face—that of politicians, artists, business executives, and heads of institutions. Such persons create opportunities for others.

The Standard Face—that of professors, bureaucrats, bankers, and businessmen.

The Workaday Face—that of wage earners, storekeepers, skilled and unskilled workers.

The Lowly Face—that of petty adventurers, riffraff, criminals, and prostitutes.

The face reader may not be able to say that you are a president of a given institution, but he can determine if you belong, say, to the third category, the Resourceful Face. This furnishes him with a good start, and he will then go on to examine each of your facial features by itself and in relation to the others. This is a complicated task, comparable to a jigsaw puzzle.

The face reader must determine which parts of the face blend with other features and to what degree. Thus if he finds that you have heavy eyebrows over weak eyes, he will conclude that you have ill-matched features, an indication of a negative character and destiny. If he finds no ill-matched features, he will examine the quality of these features in terms of strength and power and may conclude the opposite.

Let us now turn to specifics and make a study of the basic facial features, proceeding in the step-by-step manner, the best way to guarantee success.

CHAPTER 4

THE POSITION SYSTEM

THE CHINESE system of face reading is based on specific positions on the face, each indicating a specific age and each revealing some aspect of fate and personality, largely the former (fig. 7). The face reader can go straight to a given position to determine a sitter's fate or a significant event that will take place in a given year in his or her life. If a sitter tells the reader that he is thirty-seven years old, for example, the physiognomist would first examine position 37, the pupil of the left eye.

In practice, the reader is guided by the chart. It may take time to become familiar with the various positions. It would, however, suffice to memorize only the major ones. These cover the years between twenty and seventy, that is, from position 20 to position 70, normally the most important years of a person's life.

There are several schools of Chinese physiognomy, each with a different system of position. One school divides the face into 111 positions, another into 130 positions. The 100-position system I have adopted here is by far the most widely accepted. It is time-tested and accurate. In addition, to simplify the system, wherever expedient I have avoided the use of ancient, technical names, heavy with literary allusions, which would in many instances bewilder the reader and in other instances prove untranslatable.

The Position System

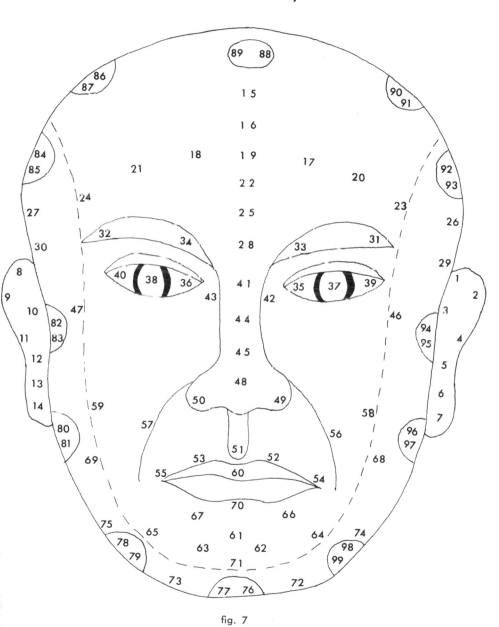

fig. 7

Perhaps the most commonly asked question is why one position designates a specific age. There is no complete answer to this question without going into the *Principles of the Five Elements* and the *I Ching,* two of the most philosophical books in Chinese literature. I have no intention of doing so since the scope of this book is limited to practical application. Suffice to say that the Position System has been handed down for centuries and is spelled out in the ancient texts. To the face reader, the most important aspect of physiognomy is its practicality. If the system has been found to work for thousands of years, that is sufficient merit to follow it today.

A glance at the chart will show ninety-nine positions (fig. 7). Position 100 is not designated because it governs the area of both chin and jawbones. As a general rule, the wider the jaws and the more upturned the chin, the better is one's chance to live one hundred years or beyond.

The central area on the chart is delineated by a dotted line drawn on both sides of the face and extending around the chin. The areas outside the dotted line cover the left and right profile of the face, as well as below the chin.

A further point. The Chinese system of counting an individual's age is different from the Western system. In China, a person is one year old from the date of birth. In the West, a person must live a full year before attaining his or her first birthday. The Chinese system is used in this book. The reader is cautioned, therefore, to deduct one year from each position number to convert it into the Western style. Thus a thirty-seven-year-old man under the Chinese system is thirty-six years of age by the Western count; and a thirty-seven-year-old man in the West is thirty-eight by Chinese reckoning. On the chart, position 37 refers to a thirty-seven-year-old under the Chinese system.

However, in terms of physiognomy the difference is negligible. Such a difference has some importance in the advanced studies of "inner energy," "seasonal changes," "skin coloration," etc., all highly involved in esoteric theories of the "Five Elements" and the "I Ching." These do not fall within the scope of this book.

Physiognomy is an art form more than an exact science.

The face reader takes this into account, realizing that what reflects in position 48, for example, may have stemmed from position 47 and may well extend to position 49. Accuracy in analyses depends largely on the expertise of the physiognomist.

Nevertheless, both numbers of the Chinese "position" age and the Western age are usually given together, especially in Chapter 17 (Photo Analysis), in order to remind the reader of the difference, whatever its validity.

As observed earlier, a beginner in face reading need only familiarize himself with the major positions (fig. 7). There are thirteen of these, extending down the center of the face (positions 16, 19, 22, 25, 28, 41, 44, 45, 48, 51, 60, 70, and 71). In Chinese lore these thirteen are known as "special positions" because they divide the face into two equal parts. If all the positions on this imaginary line are in balance and proportion with other facial features, an individual is likely to lead the good life from birth to death. The reverse is true if the features in these positions are irregular, out of balance and proportion. A quick glance at the special positions will therefore provide the face reader with a capsule summary and furnish him with a solid base for the rest of the analysis.

This does not mean that the special positions are the only important ones. As a matter of fact, the positions relating to the Five Vital Features—eyebrows, eyes, nose, mouth, and ears—are considered even more important, as we shall observe later, particularly in the study of personality and character.

Let us now explore the special positions:

Position 16 often reflects a person's relationship with parents, especially on the paternal side. Uneven, blemished surface in this area indicates unaffectionate parents and probably a troubled childhood. A dark streak in the area, especially if the streak extends to position 28, foretells an approaching disaster. Skin discoloration in this area that persists for a long period of time is a firm indication of bad luck and failure in all endeavors.

Position 19 mirrors the fate and character inherited on the maternal side. If the skin color in the area of position 19 is radiant, without any dark or dull effect, the individual is likely to receive help from a highly placed official. For that matter, any radiant color, without a dark effect, is considered a good omen by physiognomists. Blue coloration at this position points to unpleasant surprises. A yellow-red hue, without radiance, is a sign of impending misfortune.

Position 22 concerns a person's private affairs. Combined with positions 19 and 25, it constitutes the area known as the "Seat of Honors." These positions indicate the prospect of acquiring or retaining official positions, especially in government. A radiant, reddish-yellow hue in this area is the most auspicious coloration, a sign that the individual is either happily employed or is about to receive a promotion. Dark or dull skin color in this area is a sign that the individual's position is in jeopardy.

Position 25 governs a person's current fortune as well as future prospects. For good luck, the area here should be even and full without defect. Black moles signify a lack of patience and therefore repeated failures. Traces of scar tissue or a skin defect indicate trouble at the government level. If the area around position 25 is hollow and dark, it suggests a person of low intelligence. In short, if the position is full and radiant, the sitter is destined to establish himself early in life and become a dazzling success.

Position 28, or the "Seat of the Seal," is perhaps the most vital of the thirteen special positions. The archaic term "Seat of the Seal" means that this position determines a person's ability to attain a high position and social prominence.

The face reader must examine this area with care. Is the area wide or narrow? Is it clean and free of blemishes? Is the flesh raised? Is the bone structure well formed?

If the area separating the two eyebrows is wide—as much as 1½ inches—this is considered a good sign. If the area is fleshy and is marked with as many as four deep vertical lines, it indicates a person of tremendous vitality. By great vitality, the ancient texts mean great sensuality. In a person with a square or round face, fleshiness and four or more deep vertical lines reflect a high degree of maturity, both physically and mentally. Such faces are common among men but rarely found among women. Among women it indicates a strong-willed, independent, career-minded person.

Blemishes or disfigurement in position 28 indicate that the individual is unlikely to accomplish what he sets out to do. In the case of a woman, this means she will not find a suitable mate, no matter how single-mindedly she may pursue a desired companion.

Individuals with smooth skin in this area, whether men or women, tend to be feminine. In women, smooth skin indicates they are good housemakers; in men, artistic capabilities.

When the flesh in the area of position 28 is well developed and "raised" slightly, especially on a thin-set face, it suggests an individual with enormous intellectual power. The term "raised" means the swell of tissues between one fourth and one half an inch as a result of internal causes. Such raised areas, sometimes called "bumps," may also appear around the temples. In broad sunlight it is difficult to detect raised flesh, and therefore it is useful to carry out the analysis under controlled lighting.

Physiognomists attribute the phenomenon of "bumps" to inner vitality and treat them as unmistakable signs of an individual's changing fate. "Bumps" also indicate a person's maturity and reasoning power, and therefore have a strong bearing on success or failure in life. More often than not, they begin to appear in this area at the age of thirty.

In this region the face reader should also examine skin coloration. According to the ancient texts, a blackish color indicates stomach trouble; bluish, kidney disorder; red, heart trouble. A black mole at this position signifies chronic disease.

The region between positions 28 and 15 is also known as the "Luck Corridor." If the surface of this area has a hollow effect or is uneven, the individual in question is unlikely to reach a desired goal in life.

Position 41, or the "Roots of the Mountain," determines a person's fate with regard to spouse and family. If this position displays a hollow effect and is also marked by horizontal lines, it is a sign of domestic difficulties. Should the eyebrows overpower the eye and the bridge of the nose incline to one side, this suggests further adversity, ranging from grave illness to imprisonment or death in the middle years. In such cases, if other vital features are in balance and proportion, if facial coloration is bright and the voice resonant, the adversity will be softened appreciably.

Position 44 is attuned to the middle years. A wrinkle in this area indicates poor luck. A darkish coloration, however faint, indicates serious illness in the family. A mole at this spot foreshadows complications with the opposite sex.

Position 45, if there is no break in the bone structure and the skin coloration is radiant red, points to good fortune. A break or dull coloration indicates the reverse.

Position 48 reflects the vital years of a person's life. This position should be fleshy, well rounded, and healthy looking, preferably light red in color. A good shape without a healthy skin color means frustration and/or failure. Blackheads and other blemishes at this position suggest financial disaster.

Position 51, is *Jen Chung* or the "Middle Man," which governs the probability of offspring. If the groove in this area is not straight or does not occupy a central position relative to the upper lip, the individual will die without issue.

Position 60, in balance and proportion in a closed position, suggests a person with strong willpower. When the two corners curve upward, it is a sign of financial and commercial success. If the mouth opens and closes without awkwardness, it portends an expansive mind and catholic tastes. Radiant red lips augur well for the future.

Position 70 is determined largely by color. If the region is dark the individual is advised not to travel. If the coloration is red, white, or blue and lacks radiance, the sitter is warned against becoming the victim of foul play.

Position 71 controls questions of toil and treachery. If the tip of the chin is pointed, it indicates endless toil and poverty. If the chin is pointed and tilts to one side, it suggests the individual would repay kindness with treachery. Radiant red at this position foreshadows a happy event; a misty red color forecasts disaster accompanied by fire.

The other position numbers on the chart, relating to the

Five Vital Features, will be taken up in other chapters.

The important consideration, which must be repeatedly emphasized, is that the face reader must weigh, correlate, and analyze the facts collected by a reading of each position before drawing a conclusion about the person's fate and character. The reading of a single feature cannot tell a complete story about a person any more than the reading of a single chapter can tell the whole story of a book.

CHAPTER 5

THE FIVE
VITAL
FEATURES

OF ALL the features composing a human face, the ancient Chinese physiognomists considered five vital to face reading. These were eyebrows, eyes, nose, mouth, and ears. They were known in ancient texts as the Five Vital Organs. Significantly, after centuries of usage, this term is still applied to these features.

Each of these reveals something about personality. Each also governs a certain area of destiny. Among face readers, a major problem is that these features tend to overlap in the sense that there is an interrelationship among all the features of the face, and a composite reading is essential for total analysis.

Once these different features are properly understood, evaluated, and analyzed, the face reader moves on to the other related facial features such as forehead, temples, cheekbones, jawbones, and wrinkles. Finally, the practitioner turns to a reading of skin colors, the most subtle and most difficult part of the system to master.

Ancient physiognomosts maintained that if any one of the Five Vital Features is of superior shape and quality, then at least ten years of good luck are assured. And if all five features are of a superior character, the sitter will enjoy a complete life of honor, prosperity, and happiness. But there is hardly a person alive blessed with the "perfect face."

The ancient writers also maintained that if any one of these five features is not properly formed, it indicates a fissure or weakness at some point in an individual's personality makeup. An improper feature is also a reflection of an improper mind. Thus the face reader's job is to delve into a person's inner life by reading what is revealed on his face.

It is relatively easy to read the superior, well-proportioned, balanced face. It is correspondingly more difficult to analyze the inferior face with its improperly shaped features, as in the case of most of us.

The study of imperfect features therefore receives the greater part of the physiognomist's attention.

CHAPTER 6

THE
EYEBROWS

THE IDEAL eyebrows are broad, long, and elegant. They are spread out like a crescent above the eyes. The hair of the brow is full and without defects. A well-balanced development of the brow in shape, texture, and color indicates a person's emotions, intelligence, and artistic character. Such a person is in a serene state of mind. The opposite is true for individuals whose eyebrows are coarse and uneven. Such brows indicate a lonely soul, a mean, dispirited disposition, and a disturbed state of mind.

According to ancient Chinese physiognomists, the eyebrows also reflect a person's relationship to his close relatives. Elegant eyebrows indicate a person in harmony with society, more often than not a member of the Establishment. Such a person is apt to make friends and friendships readily. But the elegant eyebrow is the ideal, and most eyebrows—like other human facial features—come in a mosaic of patterns.

fig. 8

If the relatively thinner outer end of the brow bends upward (fig. 8), it indicates a person of courage and heart.

When the relatively thick eyebrow bristles upward at the outer end (fig. 9), it indicates a brave and generous character, a person with an enterprising spirit. Such a person is "born to success." However, if such a brow is of rough texture it also reveals a relentless and cruel nature.

fig. 9

A drooping brow (fig. 10) signifies a shy and cowardly nature. This type of eye brow, when the subject's texture and coloring seem lifeless, reflects the near-exhaustion of inner vitality.

fig. 10

The long, elegant eyebrow (fig. 11) generally indicates a person with a marked aptitude for longevity, honors, and prosperity. It indicates a peaceful temperament, a dislike for radical change. It points to an individual in harmony with his or her environment, someone endowed with a rich inheritance or independent income. Such a person may be an artist or a scholar. In the case of a woman, long, elegant eyebrows indicate that she is apt to be unsuccessful in marriage. However, she has extraordinary ability, and in the event of marriage failure she is capable of leading a strong, independent life.

fig. 11

If the eyebrow is longer than the eye and has an elegant texture (fig. 12), it indicates a person of superior intellect. However, long, thick eyebrows generally indicate warm family relationships and a dependable character, especially in time of need. In a woman, exceptionally long eyebrows—longer than required to balance the eye—indicate marital incompatability.

fig. 12

A short eyebrow (fig. 13) indicates almost all the opposite characteristics of the long brow. If an eyebrow is too short and thin to balance the length of the eye, it indicates that the individual is fighting a lone battle in life. If a short eyebrow has a rough or uneven texture, it points to a person with a check-

fig. 13

ered career. The short, thin eyebrow is an indication of an amorous nature and a happy marital life. But if it is too thin, indeed nearly invisible, it indicates craftiness and sensual debauchery.

fig. 14

If the eyebrow is short and thick (fig. 14), it belongs to a person with a strong sense of family loyalty, a person with an independent, aggressive spirit. This is the individual who accepts challenge, the proverbial trailblazer or pioneer. Short, thick eyebrows also identify a person with an explosive nature, capable of ardent love as well as fickleness. Finally, individuals of this type are capable of great surprises and overnight success. In this case, however, the short, thick brows must balance well with the cheekbones, eyes, and nose.

fig. 15

Short, thick, rough, dense eyebrows (fig. 15) indicate a perverse and evil personality. If the eyebrows are woolly and in layers, they point to a licentious, sex-driven, and possibly sex-depraved person.

Very short eyebrows, with a bushy, coarse texture that overshadow weak and almost lifeless eyes, are clearly a warning of instability. Such a person may be extremely dangerous. Should the thick, coarse eyebrows be surrounded by skin of dark coloration, this indicates a person of criminal tendencies.

fig. 16

When part of the eyebrow runs in the reverse direction (fig. 16), the person is likely to be stubborn. Such an individual is inflexible and uncompromising in dealing with his immediate family, friends, and business associates.

fig. 17

When two eyebrows join closely with each other to form a horizontal line (fig. 17), it often indicates a person in adverse circumstances, at the ages of thirty to thirty-five, especially if the brow hair is so stiff as to bunch up at the outer end. Such eyebrows reveal determination and resourcefulness.

A brilliant black mole imbedded inside the eyebrow (fig. 18) indicates a very high degree of success, especially in government.

fig. 18

In similar fashion, eyebrows set higher than ordinary (fig. 19) are a sign that such a person is well qualified to run for elective office or to hold a major appointment in government. If one or two eyebrow hairs stand out, it is also an indication of longevity.

fig. 19

Broken eyebrows (fig. 20) indicate a treacherous, deceitful person.

fig. 20

Eyebrows that are linked and form a thick, heavy bar (fig. 21) sometimes suggest that the subject has a straightforward nature and is unconcerned with the opinions of others. A woman with such eyebrows invariably has an extraordinarily strong character. She is apt to be unfit for the traditional role of housewife. Her marriage may end in divorce or widowhood. A woman with such brows is apt to have a brilliant professional career, however.

fig. 21

Eyebrows set in the shape of a boomerang (fig. 22) indicate a strong and resourceful nature. Such persons are capable of translating ideas into action. A woman with such eyebrows will be the prime mover in a love affair. If marriage results from the affair, she will be the dominant partner. Such women often have strong sex appeal. Sex aside, individuals with this shape eyebrow have a powerful degree of self-confidence and pay little heed to the advice of others.

fig. 22

Two eyebrows set apart in a diagonal fashion, as if converging on the middle of the forehead but not touching it (fig. 23), indicate that the subject has imagination and foresight, and the guts to take risks. In a woman, however, such eyebrows are apt to compromise her beauty in early life, even though she

fig. 23

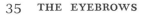

might succeed in her career in later years. This type of eyebrow creates the effect known as the "weeping face." The important clue here is that the eyebrows should not join each other in the middle. Should the space between the eyebrows contain hair, it would indicate that the person is extremely unlucky.

In addition to the eyebrows, the browbone is also a critical factor, particularly in determining a person's courage, resourcefulness, and intelligence.

fig. 24

If the browbones are very low, success in life will come late, providing the eyes, nose, cheekbones, and jawbones are well proportioned and balanced. High browbones with long, and relatively thick browhairs (fig. 24) are unmistakably the sign of a person whose browbones stand high above the eyesocket is usually successful; the mediocre have a flat browbone covered with a variety of uninteresting browhairs. However, not all high browbones are necessarily positive. For example, if the bones thrust forward in the manner of a hominid or primitive caveman, it is indicative of a cruel, violent, tempestuous nature. In women this indicates a successful professional career and an unsuccessful marriage.

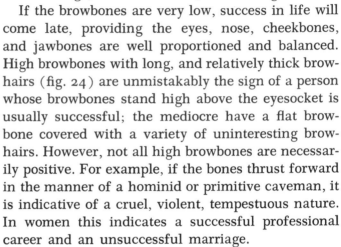

CHAPTER 7

THE EYES:
GLITTER

CHINESE face readers believe that the eyes are the windows of the heart, the eyes bare one's soul. Indeed, the eyes are probably more closely related to a person's inner vitality and personality than all other facial features combined. All the ancient texts agree that the eyes are also the most sensitive barometer of an individual's feelings. Because a person's character and spirit can be read in the eyes with the most astonishing accuracy, the face reader first examines the subject's eyes. Yet they are the most difficult of the Five Vital Features to read because they are the most subtle.

Traditionally, the best eyes are recognized by several outstanding characteristics.

First, they are elegant in shape, well positioned and well balanced not only with each other but against other facial features. Neither the eye nor the eye socket show any defect.

Second, they are usually narrow and long or large and round, and well protected by matched eyelids —that is, by the upper and lower lids.

Third, the irises are well centered and meet the eyelids both above and below. By well centered the Chinese mean as the irises are viewed against the white of the eyeball.

Fourth, the irises are clear and steady.

Finally, the ideal pair of eyes has "glitter"—that is, they reflect inner vitality and well-being. They are also fully controlled and stabilized.

These, then, are the guidelines. They set the standards for ideal eyes. Few people have them. Of the different guidelines, perhaps the last is the most important and probably the most difficult to explain, especially in the West.

Glitter refers to the "life" of the eye. Without glitter, the eye would seem glassy, spiritless, lacking in fire. An individual's ability to concentrate his gaze is a measure of "control" and "stability." These qualities reveal an individual's reserve power, his glitter or inner vitality. All human beings share an ability to concentrate their gaze, but they do so with varying degrees of effectiveness. Glitter that emits concentrated and penetrating rays indicates a person of powerful character. Whether the personality is constructive or destructive depends on the relationship of the eyes to the other features of the face, including the forehead, eyebrows, nose, cheekbones, and so forth. When glitter is constructive, it is termed controlled. As a corollary, destructive glitter is uncontrolled. Both controlled and uncontrolled glitter also reflect a person's inner vitality.

To read a person's glitter requires the ability to separate controlled glitter from uncontrolled. An individual with controlled glitter can fix a sustained, penetrating, and powerful gaze on you. He can make you feel within his power, almost exercise a hypnotic effect. On the other hand, uncontrolled glitter is often equally penetrating, but it is also furtive and scattered. Uncontrolled glitter lacks concentrated power. This type of glitter belongs to persons of mercurial character. They are unreliable by nature, people who often destroy their own careers and their family life. In theory, such a person, because of his temperament, is apt to be foolhardy, fanatical, or adventurous and may direct or misdirect his inner vitality in a manner detrimental to himself as well as to others. The following chart is a compact guide to an understanding of the Chinese conception of glitter:

Group No.	Glitter Type	Other Facial Features	Personality Traits
		GLITTER CHART	
1	Controlled	Very favorable (well proportioned and in balance)	Stable, reliable, trustworthy, loyal, an "achiever" in life
2	Uncontrolled	Favorable but irregular	Unstable, erratic, emotional
3	Uncontrolled	Unfavorable (defective)	Untrustworthy, villainous, treacherous
4	Uncontrolled	Weak and poorly balanced	Weak, easily victimized, and, hence, unlucky

Let us now analyze each of the four glitter groups in detail.

Group 1, as indicated above, consists of the best possible combination of features for an individual's eyes. Such a person has an aptitude for high positions of authority, usually between the ages of thirty and sixty. He is likely to be aggressive in character, farsighted and well organized. He goes about his affairs systematically and with an air of confidence.

A less active or aggressive individual in Group 1 usually has less powerful eyes and lower concentration power, even though the eyes are well controlled. Such persons almost never exercise their full powers directly. Frequently academics, writers, and artists are found among this type.

Persons in Group 1 can usually be trusted to play fair. They have a sense of proportion and balance. They have a benign character and a strong sense of morality. A word of caution, however: Group 1 is readily confused with persons who belong to Group 2.

Group 2 embraces individuals whose glitter is uncontrolled but is in balance with other facial features, although their features may be irregular or of mixed quality. They are given to unsteady glances, an indication of unsteady character. In other words, a person's inner vitality is so exposed to external influences, darting from object to object, as to lose self-control. Such individuals are usually impetuous.

In Group 2, however, if the eyes and other facial features appear well balanced, the indication is that the person may rise to power or influence meteorically. This is especially true of revolutionaries and adventurers. But such persons are prone to end in failure or personal disaster.

Group 3 indicates uncontrolled glitter matched with poorly balanced but strong facial features. This type of person is given to wild glances. His eyes lack reserve power. A person of this type has ability and energy, but because of impatience he has a tendency to become increasingly frustrated and therefore aggressive. Such an individual is a gambler in life. One further note: A person in Group 3 with low, protruding cheekbones and an uneven nose bridge is apt to be narrow-minded, unruly, mean, and villainous.

Group 4 covers persons whose glitter is uncontrolled and is matched not only by poorly balanced features as in Group 3 but also by weak features. By weak, Chinese physiognomists mean that a person's facial features lack firmness, appear bony, or are based on small bone structure. A person of this type is usually of weak character, a pathetic figure easily victimized by others. Such individuals are invariably unsure of themselves.

With an understanding of the four different glitter groups, we can turn to specifics. This requires a systematic breakdown of eye characteristics. First, we will make a distinction between large and small eyes, then, in sequence, focus on irises, the color of the iris, the problems of balance and proportion, the eyelids, the eye corners, and the shape of the eye. Each reveals a facet of personality and fate.

CHAPTER 8

THE EYES: EYE SHAPES, IRISES, AND EYELIDS

LARGE EYES (fig. 25) are proportionately larger than the norm. Large eyes suggest a sensitive person of courage, charisma, and leadership. Persons with large eyes are frequently found in high, responsible positions of power. People in the theater are often endowed with large eyes. In particular, women with large eyes are esthetically inclined. Usually they are not good homemakers. When a woman with large eyes has moist eyes as well, it is an indication that the woman is in love. People with large eyes usually attract the opposite sex, although the results may be disappointing.

fig. 25

Small eyes (fig. 26) are proportionately smaller than the norm. Small-eyed individuals are often not overly articulate. They tend to be introspective and avoid exhibitionism. Small eyes also mark complacent and stubborn people. Many scholars and artists have small eyes. In women, small eyes indicate a chaste, unapproachable person. Once their hearts are won, they remain steadfastly loyal. Women with small eyes are apt to have a jealous nature.

fig. 26

41

fig. 27

Persons with large irises (fig. 27) are usually gentle, calm, sympathetic, and conservative in character. Although adverse to change, these individuals are adaptable to their surroundings. However, their lack of adventurous spirit makes them unsuitable in an emergency, when they are apt to make bad decisions. Persons with large irises, whose glitter is powerful and whose eyes are poorly balanced with other facial features, are potentially cruel and heartless.

fig. 28

Individuals with small irises (fig. 28), particularly men, tend to be dissatisfied with their station in life. They are often grumblers and malcontents, unable to cope or accept the Establishment. They eventually become outcasts or loners. Such persons are often cruel and would not hesitate to use force to reach their goals, especially when they have what the Chinese face readers term "three-white-sided" eyes (See figs. 53 and 54). Individuals with small irises set in small eyes are generally small-minded people, unsteady and unreliable.

Another factor in analyzing the iris, which is not illustrated, is color. Irises, of course, come in different colors. The black and greenish-brown variety is considered a sign of inner vitality. They surpass blue irises because of their ability to adjust themselves to darkness. Those who have black or greenish-brown irises are more courageous and adventurous in temperament than people with blue irises. They are also more sensitive to colors. Individuals with light brown irises are usually shy.

fig. 29

Balance and proportion play a large part in Chinese physiognomy, as noted earlier. Accordingly, the two eyes should be on a level (fig. 29), neither eye slanting upward nor downward. This means they are in good balance. Perfectly matched eyes indicate a character of honesty, good-naturedness, conscientiousness, and serious-mindedness. Successful people, well attuned to society, have eyes in good balance and proportion.

Eyes that slant upward (fig. 30) indicate that the individual is sensitive, courageous, opportunistic, and decisive. If the person's other facial features are poor—for example, a low forehead or crooked nose —then these traits of character are likely to be employed in negative fashion. In a woman, this portends an unreasonable, jealous, and violent personality.

fig. 30

People whose eyes have a downward slant (fig. 31) are probably good-natured, optimistic, and ingratiating. They are generous and considerate, especially toward the opposite sex. They are also easily victimized. Such individuals have what is sometimes called a "weeping face" because the eyes give the impression of sadness. Such a face may damage the person's self-confidence and increase his dependency on others.

fig. 31

An upper eyelid that droops in the middle (fig. 32) is a sign of maturity, especially among relatively young people between the ages of thirty and forty. According to the Chinese texts, such eyelids suggest "ripe age" and a large degree of acumen. Individuals of this type are warm-hearted, especially if the nose is straight and full and the chin is broad and round. In matters of self-interest, persons with drooping eyelids may prove to be crafty and even callous. In no case will they ever lose sight of their own interest.

fig. 32

If the whole of the upper eyelid droops a little (fig. 33), it signifies a person with sex appeal. Such a person is apt to be cold-hearted, full of artificiality, and preoccupied with love affairs.

fig. 33

fig. 34

An upper eyelid that droops from the middle to the corner (fig. 34) usually belongs to a pessimist, a person lacking initiative and prone to be influenced by others.

fig. 35

Among men, a general drooping of the lower eyelid (fig. 35) is a sign of impotence. Among women, it signifies warmth and femininity. Such women make great lovers. But if the lower eyelids are blackish in coloration, this could indicate a woman with gynecological trouble.

fig. 36

A lower eyelid that droops toward the right or left (fig. 36) points to an individual with a strong sex drive.

fig. 37

A swollen effect in the middle of the lower eyelid (fig. 37) reveals a person of good disposition. Such a person, however, will also be egocentric and lacking in drive.

fig. 38

Lower eyelids, darkish in color, swollen and sagging in the middle or to one side (fig. 38), show impotence. This is often the result of an uncontrolled, passionate sex life in youth.

fig. 39

Swollen eyelids, both upper and lower (fig. 39), indicate that the individual is growing tired of life. Such a condition is frequently found in older people. These individuals are losing a sense of purpose and lack drive and ambition.

fig. 40

Hanging eye pouches (fig. 40), especially between the ages of thirty and fifty, are an indication of excessive sex life. Above the age of fifty, however, this is a natural sign of the aging process.

Tiny crosses located just below the lower eyelid and extending to the outer eye corner (fig. 41) indicate a suicidal tendency. Such a person is quarrelsome. At the same time, blue veins around the lower eyelids presage imminent misfortune.

fig. 41

When the outer corner of the eye—the corner near the temple—is long and pointed (fig. 42), it is a sign of intelligence and astuteness. This is mostly associated with people who are artistic, fickle, and ruthless.

fig. 42

If the outer corner of the eye points upward (fig. 43), it indicates courage, even recklessness. Such an individual is also resourceful and greedy (see also fig. 30).

fig. 43

If the corner of the eye points downward (fig. 44), it signifies a person of pessimistic nature. Such an individual may also have a submissive personality (see also fig. 31).

fig. 44

Thus far we have concentrated on the size of the eye, the iris, and the eyelid. An equally important factor for determining character is the eye shape. For easy reference, Chinese physiognomists associate a certain eye type with a certain animal.

Experience has shown that certain animals are associated with certain natures and that this is carried over in humans who may have the same facial characteristics as the animal in question. This, of course, is the approach adopted by Aristotle about 2,500 years ago; Chinese face readers are in full accord.

The ancient Chinese physiognomists classified thirty-nine different human eye shapes as relating to a specific animal. To simplify the system I have reduced the number to fifteen basic types and seven rare types, as follows:

fig. 45

Dragon's Eyes (fig. 45). These are fairly large, powerful eyes with beautifully-shaped single eyelids that usually remain half-closed. The irises are clearly defined, possessing glitter. Such a person has charisma and a sense of authority. Dragon's eyes are commonly found among rulers and great figures in history.

fig. 46

Phoenix's Eyes (fig. 46). Long eyes with double eyelids and small fishtails pointing upward and downward. The irises are usually on the dark side, with strong luster. This elegant type is found among individuals with a talent to head large corporations and institutions. Prominent scholars and artists also usually have this eyelid pattern.

fig. 47

Lion's Eyes (fig. 47). Large eyes with multiple eyelids, both upper and lower. Persons possessing such eyelids have a high sense of justice and are destined to command armies or head huge business empires.

fig. 48

Elephant's Eyes (fig. 48). Narrow, long eyes with double or triple eyelids that rarely open wide. These eyelids are found among large, corpulent people. Such people are calm and friendly, slow thinking and methodical. Women with such eyes, especially if they possess small bloodshot irises, are unusually passionate.

fig. 49

Tiger's Eyes (fig. 49). Eyes fairly round with a yellowish tint and powerful luster reveal an impulsive and cruel character. Persons with tiger's eyes usually win high honors and attain high positions in government.

Sheep's Eyes (fig. 50). Long, narrow eyes with three layers of skin on the upper eyelids. Often the irises are too small to balance the white of the eyes and are therefore blackish-yellow in coloration. Individuals who possess such eyes have sharp glitter, but the glitter is scattered and uncontrolled. These eyes belong to self-destructive persons or to persons susceptible to violent death.

fig. 50

Horse's Eyes (fig. 51). Triangular eyes with sagging eyelids. They produce a sad appearance, especially if set in a thin, heavily wrinkled face. Such eyes indicate clandestine love affairs and fickleness. Women with such eyes are highly emotional and often hysterical. Both men and women with Horse's Eyes are apt to be accident and/or disaster prone.

fig. 51

Hog's Eyes (fig. 52). The upper eyelids of these eyes are broken or point upward near the eye corner. Irises are dull, often a darkish color. A person with such eyes has a coarse, cruel character. Such individuals are often in trouble and may be victims of sudden disaster.

fig. 52

Wolf's Eyes (fig. 53). The irises are relatively small in contrast to the white portion of the eyeball at the top, right, and left. This type eye is known among Chinese physiognomists as the "three-white-sided eye." Such an eye reveals an evil personality. Individuals of this type are generally cruel, vindictive, and merciless, and they often meet violent deaths.

fig. 53

A related type (fig. 54) is the individual with the Wolf's Eyes in a reverse position. This is known as the "three-white-sided eye in reverse." The small iris is surrounded by the white portion of the eye at the bottom, left, and right. This type suggests an unscrupulous person, conspiratorial in nature, capable of violence and cruelty. Such persons are often potential murderers. According to the ancient Chi-

fig. 54

nese texts, if a forthright, honest person has an eye of this type it indicates that he will be a victim of violence, not a perpetrator.

These two eye types must be scrutinized carefully with the subject's other facial features before drawing a conclusion. In assessing the "three-white-sided" classification, the face reader must examine the subject's eyes at eye level to avoid a false reading (see fig. 28).

fig. 55

Snake's Eyes (fig. 55). The iris is small and gives the impression of "swimming in a sea of white." Often the iris is reddish in hue. The glitter is uncontrolled. This type of eye is also known as the "four-white-sided eye" when viewed at eye level. As in the case of Wolf's Eyes (figs. 53 and 54), a person with this type of eye often has a violent temper. Outraged, such individuals are given to assault.

fig. 56

Monkey's Eyes (fig. 56). Small eyes with double-lower eyelids and black irises usually identify this type. Such persons are unsteady and not in harmony with their environment. They are restless and have an unstable temperament.

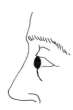

fig. 57

Crab's Eyes (fig. 57). The eyeballs protrude noticeably, much like those of a carp or goldfish. The irises often lack strong glitter. These are the signs of a stubborn, courageous, and ambitious personality. This type of individual thinks artistically but often with "twisted logic." A woman with such eyes prefers a domesticated life and is an affectionate spouse.

fig. 58

Cat's Eyes (fig. 58). Eyes with double eyelids and dark yellow irises. These eye types are strongly attractive to the opposite sex. They often convey a morbid impression that evokes sympathy in others. A person with cat's eyes is usually unreliable and has a negative personality. His or her character remains hidden, however, and the individual is generally considered attractive by an unsuspecting society.

Chicken's Eyes (fig. 59). This type of eye is also known as "wheel eyes" because the irises are lined with what appear to be spoked lines radiating from the iris itself. Eyes of this type are usually blue or hazel. Especially when a large iris leaves little white area visible, such a person is highly prone to misadventure, particularly if the spokes, radiating from the center to the rim, are very pronounced.

fig. 59

Fish's Eyes (fig. 60). The upper eyelid droops at the outer corner and has a strong downward slant. A person with such eyes is likely to be unstable, although his appearance may give him an air of placidity. Such persons are slow-moving, lack vitality, and are basically antisocial. However, contrary as it may seem, such persons lead an unbridled sex life.

fig. 60

Only by a careful study of the foregoing classifications is it possible to move on to other facial features. Remember, the eye governs the years between thirty-five and forty and plays an unusually important role in assessing character and destiny. Indeed, the eyes are so important that a pair of good eyes can compensate for poor, irregular features—but not the other way around.

In summary, the face reader is advised to examine the subject's eyes first and then see how the other facial features contribute or detract from the total picture. Is the glitter, the "life" of the eye that reflects a person's inner vitality, spirited or spiritless? Is this quality controlled or uncontrolled? These critical questions are at the very core of Chinese physiognomy.

CHAPTER 9

THE NOSE

THE NOSE occupies the epicenter of the Three Zones and has special importance in face reading since it serves as a fulcrum in balancing the face. Physiognomically, it governs the years from forty-one to fifty, the years when success or failure is largely decided.

Ideally, according to the ancient Chinese annals, the nose should encompass a straight bridge, a well-rounded tip, and beautifully-formed wings. By well-rounded tip, face readers mean that the nose should not be too upturned. Thus the openings of the nostril should be concealed. In addition, in height and length the ideal nose should appear streamlined from the base to the tip. It should not incline to either side of the face, and it should be in harmony with the contour of the face and other features. Finally, the perfect nose is well rooted to its base—the tiny area between the eyebrows and the eyes. This means it should have a solid bone structure.

The ideal nose, known as the "lion's nose," is the mark of an individual with unsurpassed virility and a strong, passionate nature. A person with such a nose has a strong sex drive and can succeed in many endeavors much more easily than those who are less well endowed.

According to Chinese physiognomists, a person

with an ideal nose is likely to occupy a high and responsible position. However, it should be emphasized that the character or fate of an individual cannot be conclusively analyzed solely on the basis of one feature alone—in this instance, the nose—because it must always be studied relative to the other features with regard to balance and proportion. Of all the Five Vital Features, the nose has the greatest number of deviations from the ideal.

Interestingly, Chinese physiognomists believe that there is a relationship between the nose and the development of the lower half of the brain. The latter development is a slow process. Thus, they explain, a child whose brain is still developing has a pudgy nose.

They also believe that there is an interrelationship between the nose and the spinal column. Since the nose is not completely developed until the age of twenty, face readers reason that at the end of the double decade an individual tends to stop growing and that the lower half of his brain has attained maturity.

Another school of Chinese thought maintains that since the nose is the organ for breathing, it is intimately related to the lungs. Breathing easily through the nose, therefore, is only possible when the lungs are in healthy condition. If a person must continually breath through the mouth, physiognomists contend that this is an indication of serious trouble ahead. In substance, of course, the face reader is drawing a diagnostic conclusion. If a person is in bed and breathing heavily through the mouth, it is obvious that the individual is in "serious trouble." We must bear in mind that the system of reading personality and fate, and their interrelationship, has been developed over the centuries and therefore contains a number of conclusions which, although clinically tested, may seem quaint in our age.

The following analysis of the nose makes this patently clear.

A long nose (fig. 61) generally indicates a person with a conservative personality, often an individual who is disdainfully proud and capable of intellectual, artistic, and/or technical achievement. Such a person is unfit for business enterprises, for the commercial world. An extra-long nose embodies the characteristics of a long nose but, in addition, indicates that the person is likely to be spiritual in nature. Individuals with very long noses are often unrealistic, flighty, and speculative. However, if a person has a long, broad nose, even though it is not well supported by other features—especially the eyebrows, eyes, and cheekbones—it indicates a person of stable character, even-tempered, and destined to "live the good life."

fig. 61

A fairly long nose (fig. 62), perfectly balanced with the eyes, the mouth, and the chin, together with two deep lines on both sides of the mouth, is ideal. These elements combine to indicate a person of strong authority, good temperament, and honesty. Such persons are sexually active, proud, and mecurial.

fig. 62

The short nose (fig. 63) is usually associated with open-minded, optimistic, outgoing individuals. Such persons are apt to be loose about their sexual morals. They also dislike detail and perform their work on the basis of emotional impulses. This is the type individual who works best when given encouragement, that is, "a pat on the back."

fig. 63

The skinny and bony nose (fig. 64) is a sign the individual lacks the power of concentration. If the nose is too high in proportion to the face as a whole, the person is likely to be proud, haughty, and difficult to get along with. Such a person, in authority, invariably has problems with subordinates. This individual is lonely and is only on tolerable terms with his spouse.

fig. 64

In all cases, a bony nose with small bumps or high ridges (fig. 65) indicates a proud, stiff-necked individual. Such a person is apt to be aggressive and determined.

fig. 65

A high and very bony nose (fig. 66) often belongs to an individual who leads a lonely life. Such a nose, if it is slightly bony but with a full, flat appearance and with a long, pointed tip, also belongs to a person of great enterprising spirit. An individual of this type is adventurous and impulsive. This impulsiveness often leads to loneliness through the alienation of friends and associates.

fig. 66

The tiny area between the two eyes (fig. 67) is called in Chinese "the root of the mountain," that is, the root of the nose. This area (position 41) is important because it governs the person's probable life expectancy and whether he or she will be a success or failure in the prime years of life.

A high root area signifies a person of strong loyalty, with close family ties. It also indicates long life. If the area is flat but full, it means the person is warm and spirited and, if married, happily so.

fig. 67

If the area is broken with a sunken effect and with horizontal lines cutting across the bridge (fig. 68), it indicates poor health and possible early death. If the area is low, coupled with fierce eyebrows that overpower the eyes and with a bridge leaning to one side, it indicates that the individual will be troubled by poor health in middle years and/ or involved in crminal activity.

fig. 68

However, in the preceding case, if the general frame of the face is fairly long and straight, the person's inner vitality strong, the skin color bright, the voice loud and clear, the difficulties that confront this individual are of a less serious character. A word of caution: The broken or sunken effect can be analyzed properly only by a comparison with other facial features, especially the eyebrows and eyes.

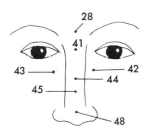

fig. 69

The bridge (positions 44-45) plays a prominent role in determining artistry (see fig. 69). The ideal bridge is high, smooth, and straight. It portends long life (see fig. 70).

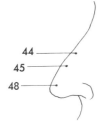

fig. 70

A person enjoying a full and well rounded bridge is highly artistic and will make a good marriage (fig. 69). On the other hand, a straight, full and well rounded bridge that extends from position 28 down to the nose tip without any defect suggests exceptional good fortune, high distinction and universal renown.

fig. 71

The area specifically governing longevity is best viewed in profile (fig. 70). If positions 44 and 45 are low and lean to one side, it means early death.

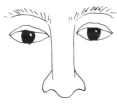

fig. 72

If the nose is narrow and looks like the edge of a sword (fig. 71), it forecasts a life of toil. If the bridge is flat, large, and well balanced by the two wings of the nose, it indicates wealth and a coldly calculating personality (fig. 72).

If the bridge is deep and horizontal lines cut across it, the individual in question is heading toward disaster (fig. 73).

fig. 73

If the bridge is broken with many small ridges, it suggests destitution (figs. 74 and 74A).

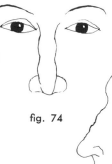

fig. 74

fig. 74 A

A bridge that widens in the middle, is covered with little flesh, and is matched with low cheekbones and small nostrils signifies a humdrum life of continuous toil with little reward (fig. 75). A woman with such a nose is destined to become a widow.

fig. 75

A bridge crossed by deep lines presages serious calamity in life (fig. 76). It also signifies a difficult marriage for women, ending in separation or divorce. If the veins are visible here, it suggests illicit love affairs.

fig. 76

fig. 77

A weak bridge (fig. 77) indicates early success and late failure in life. This is easily detected by a sunken effect between the eyes (position 41). A person with a bridge that is neither high nor low and that inclines to one side is likely to have unaffectionate children and to face constant defeats in life (fig. 78).

fig. 78

fig. 79

A high nose bridge with low and weak cheekbones and jawbones indicates birth in a socially promient family. But such a person will meet with adversity in middle years and destitution in late years (fig. 79).

fig. 80

The nose tip, like other features, comes in a variety of shapes and forms. The most valued tip is the type called the "suspending gall" (fig. 80). That is, the tip hangs in the manner in which the gall is suspended. The round shape of the tip therefore looks like the bottom part of the gall. A nose tip of this classification indicates a prosperous person with standing in the Establishment.

If the tip hangs like a lump of flesh, drooping downward (fig. 81), it indicates an oversexed nature. A pointed tip without much flesh indicates that the person has a treacherous personality.

fig. 81

A tip that looks like an eagle's beak (fig. 82) points to a person of vengeful nature. This is the type individual who has a mania about being "crossed." If, in addition, the nose tip is reddish in hue, the individual is probably unsteady, shiftless, and not given to a set career. Generally, this is known as the aquiline nose or hook nose. It indicates a person of sagacity and shrewdness.

fig. 82

Individuals with full, large, bulbous nose tips (fig. 83) are kind-hearted, warm, and spirited. They are usually self-sacrificing, but this quality must be judged in conjunction with the eyes, especially whether the glitter of the eyes is controlled or uncontrolled. The latter is a sign of malevolent nature, which compromises the individual's otherwise good nose.

fig. 83

A nose that droops and covers the greater part of the upper lip (fig. 84) is also a sign of treachery, especially when the tip is pointed and covered with little flesh. The exception here is a nose with a well-rounded tip, healthy flesh, and vivid color, even though the nose gives a drooping effect. Such characteristics offset an otherwise negative personality.

fig. 84

fig. 85

fig. 86

fig. 87

The individual with upturned nose tip, exposing the opening of the nostrils (fig. 85), usually cannot keep a secret, has loose sexual morals, prefers a Bohemian type of existence, and does not think ahead. Such a person is a free-spender who has no concept of "saving for a rainy day."

Generally, the nose tip in a man should be full and round (fig. 86). It should seem to cover a part of the groove in the middle of the upper lip. This is known in the Western world as the "Jewish nose." A person with such a nose often has extraordinary energy, boundless business acumen, and a shrewd character.

A split nose tip (fig. 87) indicates a suspicious, timid character who is rather difficult to work with. This type prefers to work out his or her problems without help. Such an individual, however, has a sense of originality and often succeeds in resolving a problem in his own way. A split nose tip is a bad sign if it is accompanied by large, badly matched eyes with three or four white sides (figs. 53, 54, and 55). In such a case, especially when the upper lip is too short, it may mean danger to his person or impending disaster.

The nose tip must be supported and balanced by the wings of the nostrils, which flare on the right and left. Wings that are well proportioned and not defective indicate that the person is probably a success in life. As a general rule, if the wings and the nostrils are large the individual is probably impoverished and unable to amass wealth. If such a person is very resourceful, on the basis of other facial features, he will have an erratic business career. Another general rule is that small nostrils belong largely to persons fit for a steady career at fixed salaries.

Nostril wings that are too flat (fig. 88), or wings that are too close to the nose center (fig. 89), indicate that a person is unable to make money and, if he does, that he is unable to keep it.

If the wings at the tip of the nose flair wide (fig. 90), it indicates that the individual is of the type to ascend from "rags to riches." This is also the mark of a sensitive, aggressive, sensual person. Such persons should be feared by slow-thinking individuals.

fig. 88

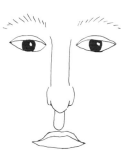

fig. 89

As for nose "color," the ideal nose should have high luster and a light red, radiant color. This suggests prosperity and high honors. Color that lacks luster and is dark signifies low birth and short life. If the area between the eyes has a bluish hue, this presages disaster.

A persistently red nose is associated with treachery, especially when the nose tends to lean to one side. A red nose usually indicates a difficult struggle for survival. A red nose studded with pores, which assumes the appearance of a spoiled orange, is characteristic of people in perpetual financial trouble, prone to licentiousness and a drinking problem.

As a general guide, a bright yellowish pink nose tip indicates "smooth sailing" in all endeavors. Strong yellowish spots on the nose tip suggest unexpected wealth. Black means sickness; blue, imprisonment; and deep red, great loss.

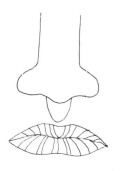

fig. 90

Reading the female nose requires special consideration. A woman's nose reveals much about her marital prospects. If her nose is beautiful, she will marry a handsome man. A blemish or disfigurement signifies the reverse. A study of the nose alone, however, cannot forecast this with precision. The nose must be studied against the background of balance and proportion relative to other facial features.

A relatively high nose on a woman, unbalanced or unsupported by low cheekbones, indicates years of misery before the age of thirty-five, because such

fig. 91 A

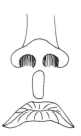

fig. 91 B

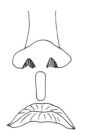

fig. 91 C

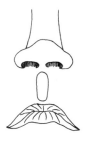

fig. 91 D

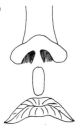

fig. 91 E

a nose overshadows the eyebrows (positions 31 through 34). By thirty-five she begins the years of the eyes (positions 35 through 40) and is likely to take a new lease on life, provided her eyes are well shaped, large, and with glitter.

A woman with a small nose in proportion to other facial features is apt to have a petty, jealous streak and suffer reverses in life. In some instances a small nose may indicate delicate sensibilities and sagaciousness.

If a woman's nose is high, with a protruding bridge, she is said to have a "man's nose" and will probably compete with man for high positions. She may marry young; if not, a marriage after the age of thirty-five is unlikely to meet with success.

Finally, the openings of the nostrils must also be closely studied in developing a composite analysis. These openings come in five basic shapes (fig. 91). The following chart illustrates the relationship between nostrils and personality:

Nostril Type	Nostril Shape	Personality Type
A	Square	Inflexible, stubborn, bull-headed
B	Triangular	Miserly, mean, stingy
C	Round	Resourceful, original
D	Horizontal Ellipse	Undistinguished, mediocre
E	Oblique Ellipse	Adventuresome, risk-taking

CHAPTER 10

THE MOUTH

IN DETECTING personality traits and fate, Chinese face readers consider the mouth one of the Five Vital Features for several reasons. The body draws air and food through the mouth, both of which are necessary to sustain life. The mouth acts as a vehicle for speech and projects a person's thoughts, providing insight into his personality makeup. And, finally, the size and shape of the mouth, in the opinion of Chinese physiognomists, assist in determining a person's inner vitality.

The ideal mouth must be shaped so that the groove situated in the middle of the upper lip is in balance with the nose and the forehead. In a man, the mouth should be strong and the lips firm. In a woman, the mouth should be delicate and the lips soft.

As a general rule, the larger the opening of the mouth, the better a person's character. But a large mouth that is unable to close tightly betrays an easy-going and irresolute personality. Such persons are often easily victimized. People born into well-to-do families without being equipped with the inner vitality for survival on their own often have mouths of this type. A large mouth in a woman indicates that

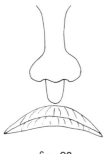

fig. 92

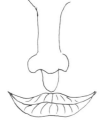

fig. 93

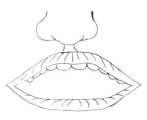

fig. 94

she has a greater aptitude for a business career than for homemaking.

A mouth with the corners in the shape of a bow (fig. 92) signifies that the person is incapable of holding high positions. A bow-shaped mouth is frequently found among persons of normal weight and those who are underweight. People falling into this category usually have a triangular face. Individuals of this type are apt to be less sensual than the average but more affectionate than individuals with a broad mouth and thin lips.

A broad mouth with radiant, red-colored lips (fig. 93) is characteristic of persons capable of exercising authority. They are responsible individuals who maintain close family ties. The same is true for persons with a broad mouth whose lips curl slightly upward at both corners.

When a mouth opens in the shape of a large square (fig. 94), with firm lips, it indicates a good-natured person. A well-centered mouth not leaning either to the left or right side of the face also indicates a happy-go-lucky personality, a person not prone to worry.

A broad mouth set on a full but firm base is associated with people of large-size bone structure. They are often self-centered, ambitious, adventurous, and aggressive. They also tend to be indifferent to their own successes or failures.

A broad mouth in a small face usually belongs to an extrovert. But if the broad mouth is on a square face, it identifies a person of authority, a good organizer. And if at the same time it is also coupled with heavy lips, a broad mouth indicates that the person is trustworthy.

As a general guideline, a small mouth means that the individual is engaged in perpetual struggle for survival. Such a mouth points to a person of weak character. Matched with thin lips, the small mouth reflects a timid character, a person fearful of assuming responsibilities. But a small mouth that opens wide indicates broad-mindedness with a touch of timidity and a tendency to procrastination.

Good lips should be thick rather than thin, angular rather than round or shapeless. Lips should be firm and rich red in color. They should be shaped in proper proportion to other facial features. Lips such as these indicate a person of integrity. When the upper lip is broad and firm, it also means longevity.

Persons with a cruel nature usually have thin lips that do not close well. Fat lips are generally associated with fat individuals. In China, physiognomists believe that such lips point to a sensually-inclined person capable of great love. This type also belongs to individuals who are orderly thinkers.

Two lips that close to form a long, straight line suggest an orderly, thoughtful, meticulous person. Such individuals are usually prominent members of society. If the line falls short of being perfectly straight in the middle, it indicates that the person has extraordinary energy and unbounding enthusiasm. As a result, unevenness in the lip line is a firm indication of resourcefulness.

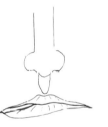

fig. 95

Viewing a person's mouth in profile, with the upper and lower lips closed, it is relatively simple to observe whether the mouth tends to protrude outward or to recede inward (fig. 95). A protruding mouth usually indicates that the person is active, decisive, and quick-thinking. The receding mouth is indicative of a calculating individual.

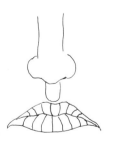

fig. 96

A firm mouth that droops at the corners (fig. 96) is known as the fish's mouth. It indicates a person of strong will, someone not easily influenced or swayed by others. In an extreme situation, such an individual will demonstrate his resourcefulness by going it alone. He or she is the type of person who "fights his own battle." The fish's mouth also belongs to the person who is an inveterate gossiper. In a woman, such a mouth type indicates a stubborn personality. In sexual relations, she is domineering and demanding. Her marriage is likely to be unstable.

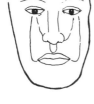

fig. 97

A mouth that twitches continually is known as the horse's mouth and is the sign of a highly nervous, tense person. The same analysis applies to individuals whose mouths are linked to the eyes or upper nostrils by distinct lines. In China, such persons are said to be destined to die by "starvation." This phrase is intriguing because it has nothing to do with a person's wealth and refers to several kinds of hunger, ranging from the psychological to the physical (fig. 97).

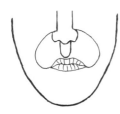

fig. 98

An individual whose cheeklines appear to be disappearing into his mouth (fig. 98) is known as a person with a snake's mouth. This classification indicates that the individual is violent, dangerous, and untrustworthy. Immediately it suggests that such a person is to be feared and may perhaps die a violent death.

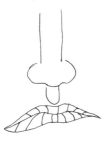

fig. 99

A person whose mouth droops badly to one side (fig. 99) is likely to be fickle and stubborn. Such an individual is inclined to use words in such a way as to offend listeners.

Often the upper and lower lips are poorly matched, one overlapping the other. A protruding upper lip (fig. 100)—which simply means a receding lower lip—is indicative of a conceited, irresolute person. Such an individual also has an insatiable libido. Such persons are often involved in extramari-

fig. 100

tal affairs. If the overlapping is in reverse (fig. 101),
it suggests a selfish individual who is likely to have
an unhappy marriage.

If the upper lip covers a large part of the lower
lip, the disfigurement is called an "eagle's mouth."
This is an indication that the individual is determined, stubborn, and possibly violent in behavior.
Such lips are more readily found among men than
women.

In some cases the outer edge of the lower lip
may curve slightly upward, especially in the middle.
In youthful persons this is an indication of a preference for a Bohemian existence.

fig. 101

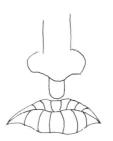

fig. 102

If the line between the two lips curves downward
(fig. 102), it is indicative of a self-centered, obsti-
nate person. Such an individual can be won over
only by flattery and cajolery. When the line curves
upward in the middle (fig. 103), however, it signifies a person who is alert and ingenious.

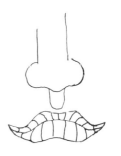

fig. 103

In women, the mouth line that appears to project
an enigmatic smile at the two corners is an indication of a deeply sensual person. Chinese face readers
call this lip formation the inverted crescent (fig.
104). It is fairly common among beautiful women.
Such women make good partners in married life.
Men rarely display such lips and, if they do, it is an
indication that they have a soft, feminine temperament and are artistically inclined.

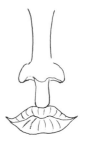

fig. 104

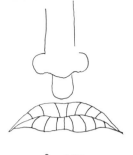

fig. 105

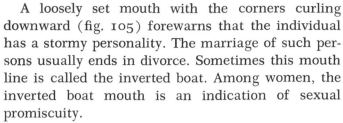

A loosely set mouth with the corners curling downward (fig. 105) forewarns that the individual has a stormy personality. The marriage of such persons usually ends in divorce. Sometimes this mouth line is called the inverted boat. Among women, the inverted boat mouth is an indication of sexual promiscuity.

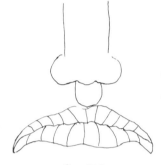

fig. 106

A broad mouth in which the corners droop downward and the lips have coarse edges (fig. 106) usually suggests a troubled personality.

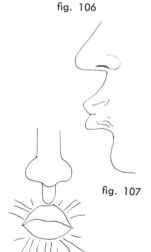

fig. 107

When the lips are thin and do not close well (fig. 107), the person probably lacks the drive for a successful career. Lips that do not match well when closed are widely regarded as a sign of criminal tendencies in an individual. In this type, when the mouth is closed it appears to have no corners because the lips expose themselves in a tight formation.

fig. 108

A person whose mouth looks like a deflated bag and is surrounded by deep lines along the exterior of the two lips (fig. 108) is probably unsatisfied with his or her job and has criminal tendencies.

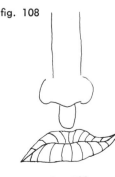

The mouth that leans to one side (fig. 109) reveals a person who is discontented and nervous. Such individuals often have a hot temper and are usually given to sarcasm.

fig. 109

A long, broad, but coarse upper lip with the lower lip small or pointed (fig. 110) is an indication that a person is gullible. Such individuals make poor business people and are easily victimized.

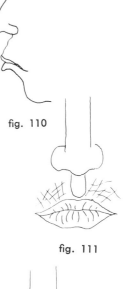

fig. 110

Wrinkles on the lips are the natural manifestation of the aging process. They can also be found on persons in poor health. But wrinkles that cut deeply into the lips and create the appearance of a weeping face (fig. 111) suggest a person who is lonely. Such individuals often enjoy success early in life and failure in late years.

fig. 111

A mouth with long, pointed, thin lips is the sign of a coward. A stiff, thick beard that closely surrounds the mouth without a break, while the lips are thin and point outward, indicates the danger of starvation as in the case of the snake's mouth (fig. 112 see also fig. 98).

fig. 112

If the two corners of the mouth appear to be poorly balanced (figs. 113 and 114), one corner seemingly higher than the other, it is an indication of a suspicious person who is also persuasive and convicing. Such individuals are untrustworthy.

A woman with a large mouth with corners poorly defined and appearing to droop is considered to have masculine characteristics. Such a woman is unfit for marriage.

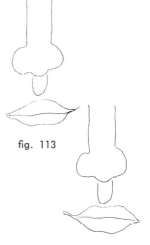

fig. 113

According to the ancient Chinese texts, an analysis of the mouth is also valuable in determining longevity. This may be summarized as follows:

Attributes indicative of a long life: A large, broad mouth in a long horizontal square with clearly defined corners. The upper and lower lips in good proportion and balance. Elegantly shaped lips with a radiant, healthy color reflecting good health and inner vitality.

fig. 114

Attributes indicative of a short life: Lips in violet or dark colors or in a deep dark color. A small mouth set against a large head. A small mouth withdrawn and twisted.

Chinese physiognomists also pay close attention to the teeth and tongue. In the first place, both relate to a person's digestive tract and, therefore, health. Moreover, if the front teeth are damaged or loose, it affects a person's appearance. A damaged tongue may also destroy the ability to speak normally.

If the front teeth are badly arranged and the mouth twisted out of its natural shape, this frequently indicates that the person will be a failure in life. If an individual is buck-toothed, it indicates he or she is incapable of concentration.

However, modern dentistry has so advanced in technique that bad teeth are no longer an insurmountable problem. How much human destiny is affected by human dentistry is a moot question. Modern Chinese physiognomists believe that a correction of bad teeth can provide a person with inward calm and happiness and, while never completely reshaping the individual's destiny, can render an improved facial appearance conducive to a better opportunity for a successful career and marriage. Thus, in its modern application, the teeth and tongue figure only marginally in face reading.

CHAPTER 11

THE EARS

LIKE OTHER complex human organs, the ear consists of many parts. The whole structure, called the auricle, is a flexible cartilage covered by skin. The auricle, like the other four Vital Features, comes in a variety of shapes.

In face reading, the ear (fig. 115) is divided into four parts: the upper rim, which folds over the upper auricle; the middle rim; the inner rim adjacent to the cheekbone, and the lobe.

In Chinese physiognomy, the ear is classified as a vital organ largely because it is more likely to indicate fate than personality, particularly in the early years. The left ear is said to govern destiny between the ages of one and seven, and to reflect the father's influence. The right ear provides clues to fate between the ages of eight and fourteen, and mirrors the mother's influence.

This is probably not as "far out" as it may seem at first glance, for between the ages of one and fourteen the fate of an individual is most often linked to that of his parents. As a general rule, the Chinese hold that a person with firm, well-shaped ears in this period has a happy childhood and a good start

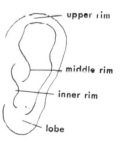

upper rim

middle rim

inner rim

lobe

fig. 115

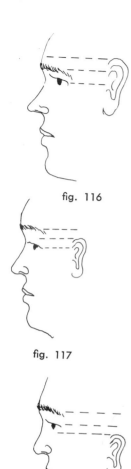

fig. 116

fig. 117

fig. 118

in life. If the ears are poorly shaped or off-color, they are said to reflect a disorganized household and a difficult environment. Unless the person has other features that are favorable and indicate that he possesses determination, spirit, and resolution, he is likely to founder in life.

As for specifics, experience has demonstrated that if the upper area of the ear is higher than the eyebrow level (fig. 116), the individual has a very high order of intelligence. Such a person is likely to achieve universal fame and/or uncommon financial success. If the upper area of the ear is higher than the eye level but not as high as the eyebrow level (fig. 117), the probability is that the person will also enjoy a measure of greatness but in a less flamboyant manner.

However, if the ear is set lower than the level of the eyes (fig. 118), it indicates that the individual is a mediocrity. In the worst cases, especially when there is no appreciable rim at the top of the ear, the likelihood is that the person is destined to have a genuinely hard struggle for existence.

The size of the ear also has great significance. Large ears are considered good if they are balanced by other factors, including thickness, softness, fine form, and radiant color. People with such ears have an aptitude for success.

But ears that are unduly large, poorly shaped, colorless, and covered by coarse skin indicate an evil personality. As a general rule, ears that are too large, and out of balance with other facial features, signify a conceited, stubborn individual.

Ears that are smaller than normal and are out of balance with the rest of the face indicate a slow-witted, dull personality. Such an individual is easily influenced by others. He or she lacks firm resolve and self-confidence. If a small ear has a defected rim, it indicates a treacherous personality. An unusually small ear, set on a person with considerable intelligence—high forehead, strong eyebrows, powerful eyes—points to an individual who is untrustworthy and prone to violence, often with a criminal nature.

Thin and soft ears, with little body, belong to bad business risks. In most instances, ears with a thin body indicate a lonely person. Soft ears, with the inside rim thrusting outward, are the ears of lustful, lascivious, sexually promiscuous individuals. If such a soft ear is bent forward, it identifies a strongly indulgent person, devoted to pleasure and sometimes lewd.

Pointed ears are relatively common, and they come in many shapes. Ears pointed at the top identify a person with a destructive personality and a low order of intelligence. If the ears are pointed and abnormally small, this indicates a stubborn, cruel character.

The rim or edge of the ear should not be defective. If the rim is small and soft, it suggests that the person is weak and lacks willpower. If it is round, smooth, and well balanced in relation to other facial features, it identifies a happy person with a fine character and close family ties. Whenever the rim (outer, inner, or middle) is clearly defined, it indicates intelligence or precocity at a tender age. Ears with badly frayed outer rims—which Westerners term "cauliflower ears"—indicate that the individual is stouthearted, independent-minded, and determined. Such individuals quite literally fight their destiny.

Perhaps the most important part of the ear in face reading is the lobe. An ear without a well-shaped lobe is thrown off balance. If the lobe is long and well-rounded, it means longevity; if the lobe is very firm, prosperity.

If the lobe is so long as to touch the shoulder (a rare situation exemplified by the Buddha), this sug-

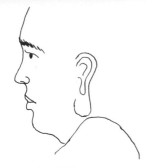

fig. 119

fig. 120

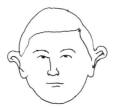

fig. 121

gests a person of superior wisdom and spirituality (fig. 119). Chinese face readers contend that such a phenomenon belongs to the nobility and to persons from unusually powerful or rich families. When the lobe turns slightly forward and upward, it also augurs well for the individual's personality and fate.

As a rule, the ancient texts contend that the less a face reader sees of the ears from a full-face view, the better. This means that the ears should lie flat alongside the head. If the ears incline backward, however, and are almost invisible from the front of the face (fig. 120), this indicates a person who is both vulgar and unfaithful. Therefore, a careful distinction should be made between the two conditions.

A person with large, soft, flappy ears that protrude from the head (fig. 121) is easily identified as difficult to associate with, particularly at middle age. If the chin of such a person is well-rounded and strong, however, he is apt to have a strong inner vitality, which may compensate in part for his difficult nature.

The inner rim of the auricle is also a major clue to personality. If it bends inward, the individual is likely to be the type that suppresses his or her emotions. If the inner rim bends outward, the reverse will be generally true.

Like other facial features, the question of "color" is a powerful factor in reading a pair of ears. A healthy red is the preferred color. A pale color, paler than the color of the face, is, however, infinitely better than red. Such an individual is likely to be a spectacular success in life. A yellow or bluish pallor to the ear is widely considered an indication of an unwell person. A dark color spreading from the ear to the temple is a sign of serious illness. Whether that illness results in a short lifespan depends upon the balance and proportion of the other facial features. In determining fate, as a universal rule, ears that have a tendency to be a shade or more darker than facial color are indicative of a negative personality and destiny.

As in the case of the eyebrows (fig. 18), moles also play a role here. A dark mole inside the auricle indicates painful litigation in middle age; a red mole near the entrance of the passage to the inner ear is a sign of longevity.

When you first take up the art of face reading, you will promptly establish certain ear patterns. For example, a stout person with a heavy-set jawbone is likely to have long, round, large earlobes. A medium-size person with thin lips often has poorly rounded ears. A person with a triangular head and a thin face usually has small, thin ears. While physiognomy may seem esoteric at this point, you will be startled to discover the accuracy between the proper reading of a person's face and his personality and/or destiny.

By way of summary, the following chart sets out the major guidelines to the ear:

Ear Type	Personality/Fate
1. Full, firm, large, radiant in color	Nobility, prosperity
2. Outer and inner rims well rounded and well balanced	Big fortunes in middle years from scratch
3. Well rounded, firm, full, close to head, positioned higher than eye level, in radiant color	Ideal type for a very successful career
4. Relatively small rims, almost invisible from front	Adventurous type, high positions with authority
5. Outer rim in a flyaway posture, central auricle sticking out	Endless toil, no help from others, never earns much
6. Without inner rim, general frame drooping forward, lobe poor	Violent events in later life
7. Outer rim flat and wide open, inner rim seems in reverse, whole ear positioned low	Trouble with the law in youth, continuous poverty

Ear Type	Personality/Fate
8. Posiitoned fairly high but middle ear overgrown, overshadowing the lobe	Inability to save money, endless toil
9. Ear top relatively small, but positioned higher than eyebrow and whiter than face and lobe	Universal fame, prosperity, live to advanced age, die without issue
10. Positioned higher than eyebrow, outer rim pointed out, bent backward	Pleasant life until old age, death without issue
11. Big, round at top in a flyaway posture, lobe pointed	Low intelligence; thieves, ruffians, rogues
12. Positioned higher than the eye, close to head, outer rim firm	Noble, rich, great fame throughout generations
13. Outer rim frayed, thin, without much body	Inherited or self-made fortunes to dwindle away, poverty in old age
14. Flapper ear, inclining forward	Good life in youth, fairly successful in middle age, poor and lonely in old age
15. Positioned higher than eyebrow, full outer and inner rims, lobe touching shoulder, round head, full forehead	Nobility, high positions, live to advanced age
16. Good outer and inner rims, soft lobe slightly drooping backward	Toil, poverty, reverses in old age

CHAPTER 12

THE
FOREHEAD

IN THE discussion of zones, the forehead was located in the Upper Zone of the face. By analyzing this area the physiognomist can tell at a glance more about a person's destiny, perhaps, than about his personality. According to Chinese face readers, on the forehead is written the story of an individual's life between the ages of fifteen and thirty.

Ideally, the bone structure of the forehead should be broad and high, but it should not protrude unduly. The areas on both sides of the forehead should slope downward, toward the temple, without a sharp breaking effect. The skin should be fairly tight and emit a radiant luster.

As in the West to some extent, among Chinese face readers the forehead is believed to indicate an individual's intellectual capacity. However, the face reader must be cautious in analyzing a "powerful" forehead. As in the case of the Five Vital Features, the "powerful" forehead must be in good balance and proportion with other facial characteristics. If the forehead is so powerful that it protrudes excessively, this could mean either genius or idiocy. Such borderline cases can only be evaluated in relation to other facial features.

The forehead should be viewed in terms of its shape, breadth, height (from hairline to eyebrow), wrinkles, hairlines (front and on the two sides), and radiance or luster. The forehead should be free of disfigurement, whether the defect is natural or the result of an accident. A forehead uneven on the left side indicates the loss of the father at an early age; on the right side, the loss of the mother. Once again, as in the case of the ears, Chinese physiognomists associate "left" with paternal characteristics and "right" with maternal aspects.

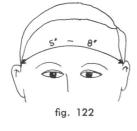

fig. 122

In determining the breadth and height of the forehead, a line is drawn one inch above the eyebrows (fig. 122). The measurement is taken from the lower right hairline, across the front forehead, to the lower left hairline. In most cases, the line is between five and eight inches in length. There are, of course, narrower and wider foreheads, but they are considered "irregular."

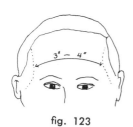

fig. 123

Ideally, the breadth of the front forehead is between three and four inches (fig. 123). It then slopes toward the temples on either side of the face. The inclination of the slope should be gentle. Individuals with such foreheads are apt to be successful and prosperous. Should there be a sudden "break" in the slope, it would indicate poverty and misfortune. A wide forehead, with a high hairline and full flesh to match the bone structure, suggests a person of intelligence and prominence. Conversely, a narrow forehead with a low hairline is an indication of mediocrity.

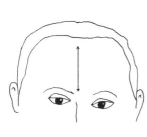

fig. 123 A

As a general rule, the hairline should be between two and three and one-half inches from the brow, but not unduly greater than the length of the nose or the Lower Zone (fig. 123A). Moreover, this length applies only to the natural hairline, not the hairline obscured by cosmetics, a wig or plastic surgery.

Many individuals begin to lose hair and turn bald early in life. But this receding line should not be considered part of the forehead.

Horizontally, the measurement of the ideal forehead should be between six and six and one-half inches across.

Thus the standard of a good forehead is an open, hairless area between five and eight inches in length and from two and one-half to six inches in width.

The hairline has much to do with the shape of the forehead. When the forehead is angular, so is the hairline (fig. 124). A man with this type of forehead is probably practical, talented, and sociable. He has an orderly, methodical mind. He is not artistically inclined, however. A woman having such a forehead has a greater aptitude for a business or professional career than housework.

fig. 124

An angular forehead with both sides of the hairline converging to make the upper hairline much shorter than the preceding type (fig. 125) indicates that the individual has an unhappy family environment. Such a person is likely to be influenced by outside pressures and is apt to be under constant mental stress. In such cases, an individual may try to correct this negative situation by adopting an assertive and bold posture.

fig. 125

The M-shaped hairline (fig. 126) is a sign of artistic temperament and great sensibility. Such a person is apt to prosper as an artist, musician, writer, or scientist. Giving rein to his passion, he probably displays inconsistent anger or pleasure. He is also indifferent to the future, has no business acumen, and prefers a Bohemian existence.

fig. 126

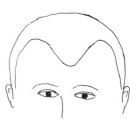

Women with hairlines similar to the M-shape but much smaller and more pointed (fig. 127) are of the chaste, virtuous type. They are feminine and enjoy

fig. 127

steady companionship. They also enjoy household duties.

fig. 128

Frequently women have round hairlines (fig. 128). This indicates a liberated spirit and an independent-minded nature. Angular-shaped hairlines can be found in resourceful, executive-type women. These women are always ready to compete with men on equal grounds.

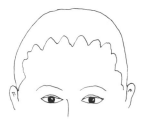
fig. 129

A hairline that is uneven and exhibits frayed edges (fig. 129) suggesting a jagged pattern is indicative of a troubled childhood and is associated with a neurotic person late in life. Such an individual is often sullen and churlish and frequently rebels against society.

Most people with jagged hairlines have inferior intellect. But, again, caution is advisable. This analysis would not apply, for example, to a person with a well-shaped, broad, and fairly even forehead despite an irregular hairline. In point of historical fact, many rebellious individuals, despite jagged hairlines, are endowed with powerful intellects.

CHAPTER 13

THE GROOVE, WRINKLES, CHEEKLINES, MOLES, AND BEARDS

As OBSERVED earlier, the human face is composed of a myriad of characteristics other than the Five Vital Features. These other features range from the groove— the area between the upper lip and the nostrils—to wrinkles, the *Fa Ling* or cheeklines extending from the wings of the nostrils to the other edge of the lips, and moles and beards.

Each of these relatively minor features should be taken into consideration in a complete analysis; indeed, without studying such features the reading is incomplete and faulty.

THE GROOVE

Between the tip of the nose and the upper lip, position 51, is the area known to Chinese face readers as the groove. The length of the groove indicates longevity. The width indicates whether a person will be childless or, if the individual has offspring, how many.

The adjectives *deep, shallow, and flat* are also used to describe the groove. Metaphorically speaking, a *deep* groove is like a canal in which water can run without overflowing its banks. The *shallow* groove is common to most people, and if it is of uneven shape the water overflows its banks. The *flat* groove, in its worst form, cannot contain any water at all, because it is ill-shaped with a flat bottom and without distinct banks.

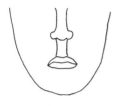

fig. 130

The ideal groove (fig. 130) is broad, long, and deep. It forecasts good fortune.

fig. 131

If the groove is narrow and shallow (fig. 131) it indicates that the sitter will suffer a serious setback at some point and will lead a life of poverty.

fig. 132

A full and flat groove (fig. 132) means a person is prone to disaster.

fig. 133

A straight groove that is narrow at the top but broad at the bottom indicates that the individual will have many offspring (fig. 133).

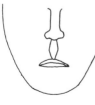

fig. 134

A diamond-shaped groove, narrow at the top as well as at the bottom but broad in the middle (fig. 134), points to trouble with one's children, in most cases serious illness.

A flat, shallow groove at the top and bottom (fig. 135) is a sign of childlessness or few children.

fig. 135

If the area is deep and long, it means longevity (fig. 136).

fig. 136

Correspondingly, if the groove is shallow and short (fig. 137), it means a short lifespan.

fig. 137

If the groove is irregular or crooked (fig. 138), the owner lacks credibility among his or her friends.

fig. 138

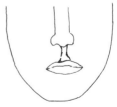

If straight and drooping (fig. 139), it signifies good luck and long life.

fig. 139

fig. 140

If a line runs across the area (fig. 140), the owner is likely to die childless.

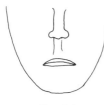

fig. 141

However, if the groove flattens gradually, disappearing near the upper lip (fig. 141), it is a bad sign. Not only will the subject not have children, but the individual will be destitute at the end of his or her life.

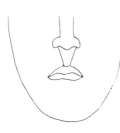

fig. 142

A groove that is broad at the top and narrow at the bottom (fig. 142) indicates the sitter is doomed to unremitting toil and poverty.

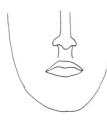

fig. 143

If the area is broadly set on a very thick lip (fig. 143), it is a sign of lasciviousness.

fig. 144

In a young person, a groove broad at the bottom, producing an upturned effect (fig. 144), is a sign of bad luck. Such an individual is unlikely to achieve his or her goals in life. In old age, however, a similar groove is a sign of good luck.

If the groove is too short (fig. 145), it suggests a short-tempered, overbearing, selfish person. Usually such people cannot hold a job for long and eventually find greater success in self-employment. A woman of this type is unfit for an independent career and is better off married.

fig. 145

An unusually short groove (fig. 146) in proportion to the other Five Vital Features is a clear sign of early death. Since the groove is designated as position 51, such a person is likely to die before reaching fifty-one years of age.

fig. 146

THE WRINKLES

Some people reach their mental maturity in their twenties, others in their thirties. In the physiognomist's parlance, this depends on his or her destiny. Usually intellectual maturity develops with experience. The more problems that challenge us, the Chinese reason, the more we are compelled to develop and use our intellect to resolve them. In this process, marks or lines appear on the face. These lines are known to face readers as wrinkles.

In physiognomy, the lines between the forehead and the chin map a person's destiny. Some lines may be quite pronounced; others, subtle. Those who live a hard life usually have deep-set lines. But this is not a certain rule since many young people prematurely acquire deep facial lines. In studying a face, an analysis of these lines can reveal much about personality and destiny.

fig. 147

There are, of course, a great variety of lines marking every facial feature. Only the major lines are studied. Across the forehead, for example, there are usually from one to six lines (fig. 147).

Irregular lines—fine, short, wavy, and scattered across the forehead (fig. 148)—indicate a lack of

fig. 148

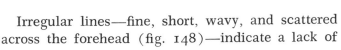

concentration, poor health, and a driftless life. Such individuals are prone to evil deeds. Even though such a person may rise to a high position, his or her mind is characterized by suspiciousness. If such lines are very deep, it may foreshadow premature death.

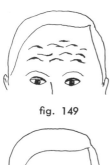

fig. 149

Irregular lines that are coarse and more pronounced and also scattered across the forehead (fig. 149) indicate frustration, sullenness, and an inability to achieve set goals. Such a person is also frequently troubled by domestic problems.

fig. 150

A single clear-cut horizontal line across the middle part of the forehead (fig. 150) is a sign of a noble life. Such an individual is likely to be successful in all enterprises, and especially at an early age. However, if the line is situated too close to the eyebrows, and therefore "too low," it may indicate misfortune early in life.

fig. 151

Two or three lines across the forehead (fig. 151) are considered a good omen. A two-line forehead is fairly common among successful, resourceful people. The three-line forehead indicates a high order of artistic and literary talent.

fig. 152

When the three-line formation is intersected in the middle by a short perpendicular line (fig. 152), it is a sign of nobility, extraordinary good fortune, long life, and a high position of authority.

fig. 153

Three long, unbroken lines across the length of the forehead in a large curved formation (fig. 153) indicate a person of great popularity. Such a person is highly respected and enjoys a wide circle of friends. This type individual lives a relatively peaceful life devoid of disaster.

Oddly shaped lines across the forehead (fig. 154) suggest early rise to prominence. However, if other facial features are weak, it signifies a destitute life.

fig. 154

A rare line in the form of a diamond (fig. 155) indicates long life and great fame. This is often found among writers, artists, musicians, and other creative persons.

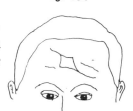

fig. 155

Between the eyebrows, at position 28, there are often two short wrinkles or lines, each slightly curved and parallel to one another (fig. 156). These lines indicate great success in government or industry, especially after the age of forty. Such an individual is probably a thinker, planner, or administrator. If other features are incompatible, he or she is nonetheless an able person who can still establish a brilliant career.

fig. 156

However, if the two lines are irregular or crooked (fig. 157), it may portend personal danger in later years.

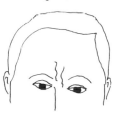

fig. 157

Similarly, if there are three vertical lines at position 28 (fig. 158), it means a person may rise to prominence early in life.

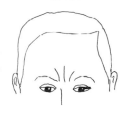

fig. 158

But if the three vertical lines are irregular (fig. 159), it means mental problems and perhaps criminal tendencies.

85   GROOVE, WRINKLES, CHEEKBONES, MOLES, & BEARDS

fig. 159

fig. 160

fig. 161

fig. 162

fig. 163

fig. 164

In some cases these three vertical lines are situated below the eyes (fig. 160). This indicates that the individual will have an unhappy marriage ending in divorce or death.

A solitary, deep, vertical line in the center of this area, seemingly dividing the face into two equal parts (fig. 161), is a bad omen. Among Chinese face readers it is known as the "Suspending Needle." This line poses a constant threat in the form of personal dangers or troubled marital relations. If the irises of such an individual are not matched or tend to display an "inverted crescent" in the lower part of the white area, and if the chin has a split appearance, the individual's life will be short. The Suspending Needle is often found among highly placed persons in government or industry. Usually, however, they have compensating features, such as ideal eyebrows, eyes, and nose. Without compensating features, the individual is clearly in unending personal danger.

So-called "Fishtail" lines, stemming from the outer corner of the eye and extending to the temple (fig. 162), signify a sly character and a crafty businessman. Such a person is in serious difficulty with his spouse and will not remain married for long. "Fishtail" lines indicate lasciviousness and frequent affairs with the opposite sex.

If the "Fishtail" wrinkle is prominent at the age of twenty, or if two or three lines point upward (fig. 163), it means the person will marry more than once and perhaps as often as three times.

Small red lines around the eyelid (fig. 164) indicate impending disaster. Since these lines are often numerous below the corners of the eyes, or near the nose, they should be examined carefully as to their color. A red hue indicates danger.

In women of child-bearing age, small lines on the upper or lower lip (fig. 165) presage the birth of a son. Such lines are without significance in elderly women.

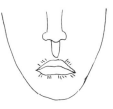

fig. 165

Two horizontal lines across the groove (fig. 166) are a sign of a low station in life, comfortable middle years, and poverty in old age.

Wavy lines below the tip of the chin (fig. 167) indicate disaster by water, perhaps at sea. So do deep, red lines (fig. 167A).

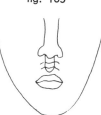

fig. 166

FA LING

In Chinese, the two cheeklines between the tip of the nostril wings (embracing the corners of the mouth and the side of the chin) are known as *Fa Ling*. These two lines, located at positions 56 and 57, govern a person's fate in the mid-fifties. These could be "crucial" years. By "crucial," the Chinese ancients mean that if an individual has led a life of failure to this point, it will be increasingly difficult to turn failure into success in ensuing years.

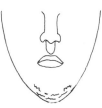

fig. 167

As a general rule, a man should have fairly prominent *Fa Ling* lines by the age of thirty. If these lines are pronounced at the age of twenty, it is clear that he is maturing early and is a self-made individual. If the lines are vague at thirty, it is a sign of slow maturation.

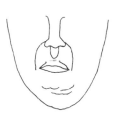

fig. 167 A

Women infrequently have pronounced *Fa Ling* lines at thirty or even forty. However, as soon as they enter competitive professional careers, these lines are apt to appear. Prominent women executives usually possess deep cheeklines. Mrs. Golda Meir, the Prime Minister of Israel, and Mrs. Indira Gandhi, the Prime Minister of India, are cases in point.

Cheeklines should be pronounced and unbroken. They should flow downward, following a natural curve. Broad, heavy cheeklines usually belong to people prominent in government or society. Deep, long cheeklines indicate longevity. Heavy, round-faced people tend to have weak, faint lines; triangular-faced persons tend toward small, fine lines; and individuals with square or oval faces usually have deep and pronounced *Fa Ling* lines.

If a person's cheeklines are pronounced but disorderly—that is, irregular, broken, or crooked—he or she may be confronted by misfortune, adversity, and danger. If the two cheeklines are of different length or are not parallel, it is possible that the sitter has a dual personality and lacks the power of concentration. When the *Fa Ling* lines are not clear-cut or of equal length, it suggests failure in one's enterprises. A mole straddling the *Fa Ling*, either right or left, forebodes personal dangers (see analysis of Lincoln's photo later).

fig. 168

fig. 169

Ideal cheeklines maintain balanced curves on both sides of the face, at a distance from the corners of the mouth. This type belongs to the average person with a fair degree of success in life (fig. 168).

Cheeklines that are straight from the top of the nostril wings to the end, although not touching the corners of the mouth, reveal a bitter struggle in life (fig. 169). Such a person is beset with continuous poverty and illness.

fig. 170

Noble cheeklines are those that begin with a flowing line in a gentle curve, fading away to the side (fig. 170). These belong to high officials.

fig. 171

When the lines end somewhere near the corners of the mouth but do not touch them, and another set of lines appear from the corners of the mouth to the chin, the individual will enjoy great success in life (fig. 171). These lines become more pronounced and deeply furrowed after the age of sixty.

Individuals with multiple folds (fig. 172) usually have extraordinary power in the political or financial world, provided their other facial features are in balance and proportion and can match these superior folds. The late Lyndon Johnson is a case in point.

fig. 172

Short *Fa Ling* lines, coupled with a thin nose, exposed nostrils, uneven lips, and a pointed chin (fig. 173), combine all the worst features in the lower part of the face. This belongs to a person in perpetual poverty, who suffers a lengthy illness and early death.

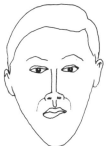

fig. 173

The *Fa Ling* lines rarely denote evil. An exception to the rule, however, is in the case of the individual whose cheeklines end directly at the corners of the mouth (fig. 174). Among Chinese face readers this is called the "Flying Serpent Entering the Mouth." Such a person is likely to end his life in terrifying circumstances (see fig. 98.)

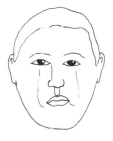

fig. 174

Another exception to the rule is when the two lines extend from the lower eyelids to the mouth (fig. 175). This presages an unnatural death. Such features call for a cautious analysis and must be studied against the whole face.

MOLES

Chinese physiognomists believe that a mole is Nature's last touch and is designed primarily to accentuate beauty in a beautiful person. But not all individuals are beautiful—hardly—and therefore most moles do not serve in this benevolent fashion.

Moles come in different types. Each mole has significance according to its shape, position, and color. Hence the ancient texts held that the most important aspect in reading a mole is its radiance, particularly those that are red or black.

fig. 175

89   GROOVE, WRINKLES, CHEEKBONES, MOLES, & BEARDS

The most common coloring of moles is gray, dark or black, usually without luster. More often than not, the mole is dull in color. This is considered unlucky. For example, if a dull-dark mole is located between the two eyebrows, in position 28, it not only mars the beauty of the nose near its roots but also impairs the good fortune that the ideal nose may portend. In such a case the face reader interprets the mole as a sign of instability or irresolution in the sitter.

Dark moles serve to forewarn misfortune in other ways. At position 25, for example, just above the eyebrows, a mole is considered an obstacle to official promotion and also a sign of repeatedly changing careers. Just below the inner corner of the eye, at positions 42 and 43, a mole is a warning of impending trouble with one's offspring. Moles at positions 44 and 45, on the bridge of the nose, suggest heavy financial losses or embroilment in an affair with the opposite sex. At position 48, at the tip of the nose, a mole denotes bankruptcy or a sex scandal involving the individual. For a man, a mole at position 51, centered right above the lips, portends early death; for a woman, it suggests gynecological problems.

At position 19 or 22, centered on the forehead, a mole indicates the loss of parents before the age of twenty-two. The individual is also destined to suffer the calamity of fire at least once in his or her lifetime. At position 41, at eye level on the nose, divorce and chronic illness are foreshadowed. At position 70, centered right under the lips, danger from poisoning is manifest. At positions 46 and 47, below and to the outside of each eye, the mole suggests the individual will be involuntarily drawn into someone else's personal problems. If the mole is on the right or left side of the forehead, above the temple, the individual is destined to fail in an endeavor at least once.

Astride the groove, a mole signifies that the individual will bear no offspring. Straddling the *Fa Ling* line, a mole on either the right or left at position 56 or 57 forebodes personal danger, such as death by fire (fig. 176).

fig. 176

In examining a mole, no matter on which part of the face it is located, the face reader is advised to analyze other facial features carefully or the reading may lead to erroneous conclusions.

To recapitulate: A mole that is radiant in color and is set in an area of light-colored skin augurs good fortune (see fig. 18). But if the mole is dull in color, the sitter should be advised against impending misfortune.

BEARDS

According to Chinese physiognomists, a young man's fate is better revealed by his eyebrows and an old man's fate by his beard. As a rule, therefore, face readers focus their attention on the eyebrows of the young and the beards of the old. However, beards have now become fashionable among young men. Even so, fashion should not confuse the face reader. Facial contours and coloration are paramount, irrespective of the beard.

In evaluating beards of the young or old, some basic rules should be borne in mind.

Good beards are on the thin and soft side and a radiant darkish color. Thick, bushy, grizzled beards, reddish or yellowish in color, are the most undesirable. An older person without a beard is regarded as "incomplete" according to Chinese physiognomists.

A bearded man should have his beard in the groove on the upper lip. Otherwise it would subject him to slander or "receiving hatred in return for kindness."

A thick, bushy beard on a government official is

likely to direct popular criticism at him without cause.

A bushy beard, coupled with bushy eyebrows and also with small blackheads around the beard, is indicative of danger related to water. A yellowish beard on a pale face, coupled with reddish veins near the beard, is a sign of danger related to fire.

A very thick bushy beard that literally seals the mouth in a watertight fashion also is indicative of personal danger. If the beard is coupled with thick bushy eyebrows and lifeless eyes, it means death from hunger. (See fig. 112.)

CHAPTER 14

CHEEKBONES, JAWBONES, CHIN

IN CHINESE physiognomy, in addition to the forehead, there are several other relatively minor facial features that must be studied together with the Five Vital Features to assure a correct reading. Among them are the cheekbones, jawbones, and chin.

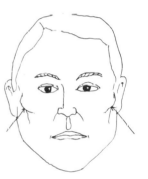

In terms of bone structure, the area that forms the eye socket and has a slightly protruding point below the eye is known as the cheekbone (fig. 177). Normally the cheekbone is set on a level with the inner opening of the ear. In face reading, the cheekbone indicates the authority a person has over others, especially in policy-making. Thus the cheekbone of a person in authority in government, in an institution, or in industry should be closely observed. Not only can an experienced face reader discern a person's true position of authority, but a sophisticated reader can tell if the sitter is on the verge of acquiring greater authority or is in danger of losing authority.

fig. 177

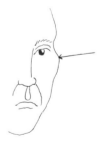

Especially when matched by a high browbone, the high cheekbone is a sign of influence and power (fig. 178).

fig. 178

fig. 179

If an individual's forehead is fairly wide and high, his eyebrows fairly strong, and his eyes fairly bright, the person is apt to lead a happy life. However, if these signs are accompanied by weak cheekbones, the person is unlikely to ever enjoy any large degree of authority. Similarly, a low-positioned cheekbone (fig. 179) accompanied by irregular features indicates a person of little or no authority.

Both the right and left cheekbones must be analyzed simultaneously for balance and proportion. If one cheekbone is lower, smaller, or out of shape relative to the other, it indicates that the person's other good features, if any, may be compromised. Therefore, bad cheekbones reflect more than a lack of authority. They also serve as a warning of a compromised destiny.

On a square-faced person, the cheekbones are often strongly developed and prominent, even striking to the casual observer. In such cases, this feature points to a fighting spirit and a desire to change the prevailing conditions of the individual's environment.

fig. 180

In a round-faced person, the cheekbones are often underdeveloped. This suggests a conservative outlook. In a long, thin face, the cheekbones are usually highly developed, but they may not project outwardly. This indicates a person with a passive character, especially if the cheekbones are set lower than ear level (fig. 180).

The flesh covering the cheekbones is a very serious consideration in reading this facial characteristic. The flesh should not be thin and stretched so tightly over the cheekbone as to render it pale. The flesh should be full and in a radiant red color, reflecting the healthy condition of the blood. A person with such skin and coloring has an aptitude for money-making and, with other good features in balance and proportion, is likely to hold a position of authority.

In a triangular-faced individual, often there is little flesh on the cheekbones. This indicates a highly sensitive and creative type individual.

Women rarely have prominent cheekbones. Those with high cheekbones are likely to be independent-minded. Such women are gifted with creative ability and self-reliance. They enjoy competing with men for careers. Women with high cheekbones usually marry and enjoy family life only in situations where their partner has a stronger personality.

In reading the cheekbones, this checklist provides a useful frame of reference:

Since cheekbones correspond to positions 46 and 47, below and to the outside of each eye, reading this feature applies to a person's fate particularly in these years. If the cheekbones are highly positioned, well covered with flesh, and well balanced with other facial features, it is a clear indication of a person of authority, the extent of the authority to be determined by an examination of other features. If the cheekbones are badly formed, not on the same level with each other, but well covered with flesh, it is a forewarning of misfortunes in middle age. If the cheekbones are too high, particularly against a receding forehead or a low-bridged nose, it means a life often fraught with personal danger. This also applies in the case of an individual whose cheekbones are too low and are set against a concave forehead or a protruding nose.

As for the chin and jawbones, they are almost inseparable and are therefore often discussed together in the Chinese texts. These two features govern the late years of life and are located at positions 60 through 79, and also 98 and 99 on the left.

Well-developed jawbones on a round or square face, matching the general contour of the face, usually indicate strength of character. In a round face, the jawbones suggest affection, generosity, and self-control, provided they are broad and are covered with firm, full flesh. In a square face, they reveal individuals with a strong resolve and a hard or difficult personality. Such a jawbone is usually associated with a professional athlete or military man. Generally speaking, however, the face reader should keep in mind that a broad jawbone and a broad chin are signs of strong character unless compromised by other poor features (such as a weak or broken nose or lifeless eyes). If a person has such a jawbone and chin, whether man or woman, the individual will probably have a very successful life if other facial features are favorable and in balance and proportion.

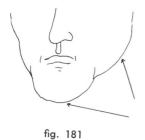

fig. 181

As a rule, the broader the jawbone, the broader the chin (fig. 181). The size and position of these two features must match well. A broad and slightly upturned chin is absolutely necessary to balance the whole face. It indicates good luck and good fortune late in life.

fig. 182

A weak or receding chin (fig. 182) is a clear sign of a fatal defect in character and destiny. From the forehead down, a weak chin places other facial features in jeopardy.

fig. 183

A strongly pronounced cleft in the chin (fig. 183), as the result of a split in the bone structure or in the flesh covering the chin, is known as the "split chin." As a rule of thumb, such a cleft points to a warm, affectionate, passionate person. It is frequently found among artists, actors, musicians, investors, and writers—that is, among individuals whose creative work generates high emotion.

However, if the "split chin" is rooted in the bone structure and not the skin, unrelieved in any manner throughout its length, and matched with defected irises and perhaps an imperfect nose bridge, it may signify an unnatural death. The "split chin,"

without other defects, suggests problems of introspective withdrawal.

In some cultures a pointed chin among women is
considered a mark of beauty (fig. 184). Such a
chin may not be fully developed and therefore may
not be fleshy. But a fully developed chin should
emerge by the age of thirty. In the event that the
chin remains pointed at this age, the face reader
usually considers this a defective feature since it
often strikes a poor balance with other prominent
facial features. Imbalance is always undesirable.
After the age of thirty, a pointed chin may suggest
frustrations, illness, and a short lifespan.

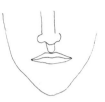

fig. 184

Broad jaws and a broad chin on a broad face (fig.
185) are the signs of a strong personality. Such
features are often found in individuals of great
determination and craftiness. Nothing can deter
such an individual from achieving his or her objective. However, a long chin, without fully developed
flesh, is the sign of the unsuccessful financial
manipulator. If the chin is flat, it indicates that the
individual is unresourceful.

fig. 185

Heavy jawbones protruding on both sides of the
lower face, and clearly visible from the back of the
head (fig. 186), indicate a person in revolt, an individual of uncontrollable passion. Such a person is
apt to repay a benefactor with treachery. Politicians,
revolutionaries, and unprincipled businessmen usually display this type of jawbone.

fig. 186

In some cases, the protruding jawbone is hidden
by a mass of flesh. This indicates a self-centered,
selfish individual. A woman with such a jawbone is
often a difficult marital partner, for she is in continuous revolt against her destiny.

CHAPTER 15

LONG LIFE, SHORT LIFE?

IN YOUTH, the typically healthy and busy person, preoccupied with life and its potentialities, rarely thinks about death. As an individual grows older, however, he becomes increasingly aware of the human lifespan and raises questions about the future. Perhaps the most basic question is simply: How long will I live?

To this question there is no easy answer.

Religiously-inclined persons who have faith in a hereafter believe death is the threshold to another world. They have put themselves in the hands of God. Others want to know how and when they will die, in an effort to foil or delay their fate. As a consequence, in ancient times, the ingenuity of the Chinese physiognomist was put to work to solve the riddle of life and death.

Chinese face readers make no pretense of supernatural powers. They are not charlatans. However, by closely studying facial characteristics over the centuries, they have detected a relationship between longevity and features.

Even so, the Chinese physiognomist hastens to emphasize that there is no foolproof way to forecast death to the year, month, day, and hour. The man condemned to the gallows may be subject to a last-minute reprieve.

Thus the fate of a person with regard to death is far too complicated to forecast with certainty. Yet there are signs, and these have been read since ancient times, although it must be stressed once again that the face reader makes no pretense at omnipotence.

Chinese face readers believe that their system of analysis can bring us very close to the truth about a person's longevity, however. This cannot be determined by the manifestation of only one facial feature, however favorable or unfavorable. A composite analysis is the iron rule.

Against this background, this inquiry shall be approached in terms of the signs of long life, short life, unnatural or violent death, and the facial features that are generally considered negative signs.

In general, a person with a face free from defects, superior in shape, balance, and proportion, is apt to enjoy a long lifespan. This is especially true if the following characteristics are present:

Bone structure—even and high from browline to hairline.

Eyes—well shaped with controlled glitter and spirit.

Cheekbones—well developed and high, matched by large ears.

Eyebrows—set high, even, long, and firm.

Groove—deep, long, and straight.

Nose bridge—straight, full, and firm.

Fa Ling lines—clearly defined and unbroken.

Chin—broad and upturned, without a long, deep cleft.

Ears—long with well-rounded lobes (this is the most auspicious sign of long life).

As for the signs of short life, they are also many in number and, as a rule, are of opposite value. The following salient factors are associated with a short lifespan:

Position 41 (at eye level on the nose)—sunken effect and blotched by darkish coloration.

Ears—thin, soft, shapeless, without outer folds, with flat auricles, and quite below normal size.

Groove—short, shallow, or crooked.

Eyeballs—protruding, glitterless, and lifeless.

Eyebrows—exceptionally rough and heavy.

Nose—crooked, broken, little flesh.

Eyes—"three-white-sided" or "four-white-sided."

By contrast, unnatural or violent death is presaged by a

largely different set of features. They are fifteen in number, and the most significant are marked by an asterisk. They are as follows:

*Three-white-sided eyes.

*Four-white-sided eyes.

Triangular-shaped eyes with the upper lids arched up.

*Wheel-eye ("chicken eye"), "sheep-eye," and the "hog-eye."

*Glitter—scattered or uncontrolled.

*Position 41 (at eye level on the nose)—a deep sunken effect with a dark bluish color.

Pupils—large, or perpetually pierced by red veins, or yellow in color.

Ears—unusually small in size.

Wrinkles—in the form of a net under the eyes (right or left).

Eyebrows—running against the grain or shooting upward like a sword.

Face—blackened when angry.

*Nose—red vein or veins running across the bridge.

Large ears—without a clearly defined upper edge.

*The "suspending needle" between the brows.

A short, thin upper lip with a very shallow groove.

In addition to these signs of long and short lifespans and violent death, there is a set of facial features that tends to forecast problems of varying intensity and complexity. These "bad signs" or ominous facial features can be easily identified. In review, they are as follows:

Head—pointed, with narrow forehead and tight skin (early death of parents and continuous failures throughout the years up to fifty).

Chin—receding, without an upturned tip (divorce, separation, or short life).

Temples and ears—sunken effect (unhealthy internal organs and a checkered career).

Face—no single clearly defined feature (mediocrity, nonentity, and useless life).

Position 41 (at eye level on the nose)—uneven and sunken (an indication of a lonely life without help either from relatives or friends).

Nostrils' openings—too wide and exposed (inability to save and marital instability).

Beard—uneven or not full enough to cover upper lip (endless toil without help from friends or relatives).

Ears—turned backward, without a clearly defined crescent (continuous losses of property and cash).

Eyes—without glitter, lifeless (poverty, frustration, loneliness).

Fa Ling lines—broken in several places or intersected by a mole (serious upsets in life, possibly personal danger).

Again, as a word of caution, the beginner in face reading must remember that the defects listed above may not be judged in isolation. They must only be interpreted relative to other facial features and constantly within the framework of balance and proportion.

CHAPTER 16

PROBLEMS OF APPLICATION

To CONDUCT a successful reading, the face reader should first establish rapport with the sitter. The reader should seek to empathize with his subject in the manner that the psychiatrist does with a patient. Only a high degree of harmony between the reader and sitter can assure an accurate reading.

If the relationship between the physiognomist and the sitter is one of nonrapport, a situation may result in which each is suspicious of the other. In such a case, the fly-by-night face reader might be able to render superficial reading. But the scholarly, sophisticated, sensitive practitioner would cancel the reading because the conditions were not suitable to make the effort meaningful and therefore successful.

The self-evident truth is that all men and women are created equal—but different. Therefore in several areas we have treated the two sexes separately in the manner of ancient texts. Although under the early social structure that emerged in China the status of women was far different than that of the "liberated" woman of today, the basic physological and psychological differences between the sexes remain unchanged. In the following paragraphs, the various practical problems that confront the reader are discussed as applicable either to both sexes simultaneously or separately.

For example, the subject of age. Many people, especially women, are wary of revealing age. Some deliberately lie about it. Without a knowledge of the sitter's age, the reading is limited to generalities. However, a reader may maneuver around this ticklish problem by asking the sitter if he or she is somewhere between the ages of thirty and forty, forty and fifty, or fifty and sixty. Then he would proceed to examine the person's features.

Face-lifting and plastic surgery are other problems confronting the reader. A person who has undergone cosmetic surgery may give a more youthful appearance, but an experienced reader should always try to get to the truth and should make allowance for hidden years.

A woman's makeup is still another hindrance to face reading. If the facial makeup is too heavy, the natural wrinkles, for example, may be obscured. A wig—now popular among men, too—may also obstruct a reading by covering the natural hairline.

Only by establishing good rapport with the sitter can the reader resolve these assorted problems. As in the case of the physician, the face reader must adopt a "bedside manner" and win the confidence of the subject.

Experienced face readers must also exhibit savoir faire in dispensing bad news. In the event of a negative reading, the reader should use caution, inform the sitter in slow stages, and prepare the subject for the bad news. However, there is no fixed philosophy in handling such a situation. Indeed, some face readers prefer "shock" treatment and disclose bad tidings immediately. They then seek to assuage the sitter. To the Chinese mind, however, this is considered too harsh an approach to the problem. In China, this is where the centuries-old philosophy of the "Doctrine of the Mean" enters—when one is strongly persuaded not to carry a matter to the extreme. In Talleyrand's words, "Above all, not too much zeal."

In the event of a negative reading, the physiognomist always retraces his steps and doublechecks his analysis. Nothing is worse than an overconfident reader who hastily draws conclusions from casual readings. The result could be tragic.

In addition to reading the face, the practitioner should automatically observe the sitter's body build (heavy or light), inner vitality (nervousness, outward behavior), voice (gentle or resonant), mode of conversation (cool, forceful, emotional), and so forth. A thorough observation of these points will enable the face reader to assess the sitter's temperament and personality, insights that aid in developing reader-sitter rapport.

As a general guideline, it is useful to encourage the sitter to talk about himself or herself. This will enable the reader to detect, by posing innocent questions, whether the subject is prone to evasion, direct answer, or exaggeration.

Systematically, thereafter, the reader can apply the lessons covered in this book—judging the contour of the sitter's face, the elements of balance and proportion among the Three Zones, the Positions, and the Five Vital Features.

As in everything else, experience makes a superior practitioner. The reading of a face, each and all of its features taken as a whole, is relatively simple, and anyone who has studied this book can do so. But it is the odd, unusual, or "irregular" face that presents a challenge. As a rule, the noble and great face and the humble and lowly face—at opposite ends of the spectrum—can be easily recognized. Those in between, individuals with borderline features, present the reader with the need for caution, experience, and genuine expertise.

The experienced face reader should be as confident of his or her analysis as the physician of his diagnosis. Remember, there is no magic formula in face reading, no shortcut.

In China the story is told of the magistrate of a district who disguised himself one day to test the expertise of a famous face reader. The man, then in his fifties, had odd facial features and appeared unprepossessing. The rank of magistrate in imperial China, however, was an office of prestige, power, and authority.

After a casual look at the official, the face reader opened with a frank statement. "Most face readers would agree that your face is of the lower order," he intoned. "You can hold no higher position than that of a dogcatcher."

Stung by the statement, the magistrate was shaken. The

face reader continued: "Please be patient as I have not yet told you my own studied opinion. When I said 'lower order' I referred to your facial features, which are badly disproportioned and ill-balanced. But I see balance within imbalance, strength within weakness. Your eyes are small but controlled. Your nose is short but straight and fairly balanced. Your ears are substandard but matched well to your round lobes. Your mouth is small but radiant in color. These features are decidedly unfavorable in appearance, but they are in balance and make a strong point in your favor. Moreover, your eyebrows match well with your eyes, indicating high intelligence. I therefore conclude that you should hold a high position of authority in government."

The magistrate departed convinced that an individual's fate can only be read in depth and that superficial facial appearances do not tell the whole story about a person's personality and destiny.

Inexperienced physiognomists should bear this story in mind.

CHAPTER 17

PHOTO
ANALYSIS

TENS of thousands of case histories, ancient and modern, are included in the files of Chinese physiognomists. They not only serve as models for beginners but enable experienced face readers to review the principles of this scientifically-based art. Of perhaps greater value, however, is the accompanying gallery of photographs that I have analyzed in accordance with the points covered in this guide. Here you will observe the practical application of theory.

The photographs were selected to assist you in identifying prominent facial features and learning how and why they affect personality, character, and fate. A word of caution: You must correlate the number in the Position System to the specific feature. Failure to do so means that you may mistake a person's character and fate, or that your reading will be based on mere guesswork. In using the Position System, keep in mind the differences in the Chinese and Western ways of counting age (see Chapter 4).

The student must also bear in mind that in Chinese physiognomy, which is an integrated system, a solitary feature cannot reveal the sitter's complete personality. Only by analyzing and weighing the values of various features—especially the variables—can the student gain the confidence and skill to make an accurate assessment and to draw correct conclusions.

Reading a photograph, of course, is a different matter from reading the actual face. A photograph is limited to the lighted and visible side of the face. Reading a person in the flesh provides the opportunity of studying the whole face, whole head, and, in fact, the whole person. Even the way in which the subject sits, walks, talks, etc., may reveal a great deal about his or her character. Lighting that permits examination of the coloration of the subject's face—and advanced study—can afford, for example, an opportunity to detect temperament and disposition.

The photographs in the following pages represent a study of contrasts, a cross-section of society that transcends race, color, language, religion, nationality, culture, and economic position. This in itself demonstrates clearly the universality of the Chinese system.

A thorough study of the faces in these photographs will offer the student a working tool with which he can apply the secrets of Chinese face reading.

ABRAHAM LINCOLN (1809–1865)

The physiognomist's first impression of Lincoln's face is that of a giant with great sensitivity and perseverance. The M-shaped hairline and powerful forehead combine to indicate a man of high ideals. There are three distinct horizontal lines on the forehead—the sign of resourcefulness, the sign of the thinker. However, the third line is somewhat disconnected on the left and others, located immediately above the brows, are broken up. All these are defects, though of a minor nature. But there are serious defects in the browbones, which are so high that they thrust the eyebrows forward and overshadow the eyes. The nose bridge, though solid at its root (position 41), is also overshadowed by the browbones. Physiognomically, all these characteristics imply imbalance and disproportion.

Nevertheless, these defects are compensated by his powerful forehead and noble face viewed as a whole. That is to say, although the defects can cause continuous frustration and disappointment before the age of thirty, they do not impair the high potentials of this face and rather indicate that greatness will ripen only late in life. As a matter of fact, from the hairline down to the nose tip (position 48) and its wings (positions 49 and 50), nothing startling in his career can be expected except some minor successes at the age of twenty-six to twenty-seven, and then again at thirty-eight to forty (positions 39 through 41)—when, indeed, Lincoln was elected to Congress.

As represented by his nose bridge, the years 40 to 49 were a series of failures. Success in his face will not begin until the age of fifty, as indicated by his groove (position 51), which is one of the most perfectly formed features on

this countenance. Coincidentally, at the age of fifty-one Lincoln emerged as a leader of the first rank, winning the Republican Presidential nomination.

The years from fifty-two to fifty-five can be read in the upper lip, which is firm and perfectly shaped. Lincoln was fifty-two when elected President. However, because of the disproportioned upper part of his face, it was fated that he would not be a peacetime President.

Physiognomically, there are other fateful features in this face. First, the eyes are of the "three-white-sided" type, which warns of danger. In Lincoln's case they are neutralized by the redeeming feature of a formidable forehead. Therefore, what might seem signs of disaster (positions 37 and 38) turned out to be frustrations and failures but without personal danger, especially in the years thirty-six to thirty-seven.

A second fateful feature is the right cheekline (position 57), which represents his fifty-sixth year. Here we find a mole to block an otherwise perfect cheekline. With these two fateful signs, in addition to a disproportioned forehead and a weak chin (though covered by a beard), this is the face of a man with high ideals who will die at the hands of an assassin at the age of fifty-six.

LI HUNG-CHANG   (1823–1901)

Li Hung-chang, a great literary figure, a high-mannered poet, a brilliant statesman and a skilful diplomat, lived a turbulent public life in the manner of Winston Churchill. In history he is known as the "Bismarck of Asia" because of his adroit juggling of the Great Powers in order to save China, then in decline under the Manchus, the last imperial dynasty.

Chinese physiognomists called him a "Man of Destiny" because the broad forehead, refined eyebrows, penetrating eyes, powerful nose bridge, and strong nose tip presaged great official responsibilities at the age of forty-eight. His moustache unfortunately obstructs a closer examination of mouth and chin. But the chin shows a broad base, without which the whole face would have been ill-balanced and ill-proportioned. By glancing at these features one cannot fail to recognize a man whose destiny was to save an empire.

The broad forehead shows that in his twenties he had already distinguished himself through public examinations. In his early thirties (positions 31 through 34) he caught the attention of the imperial court and was given the command of the Northern Army to suppress the Taiping Rebellion. From his forties (positions 41 through 58) his promotions continued. At age fifty-eight he was Grand Secretary of the Court (1881) dealing with aggressive foreign powers. Because of an inept Manchu government at Peking, he was compelled to negotiate from weakness.

His left cheekline is deep and powerful, and so at the age of fifty-seven he faced a great crisis. In point of fact, when he attained that age Japan challenged China to a war over Korea, and China lost.

The ruling Manchus sent him to Japan to sue for peace. Li had to sign a humiliating peace treaty and, as a consequence, the court stripped him of honors and banished him to a minor provincial outpost for the next thirteen years, as mirrored by the mouth and chin.

But the left lower side of the chin (position 72) indicated that at that age he would return to prominence and exercise authority. As it developed, the Manchus recalled him to office to renegotiate an end to the Boxer rebellion at the turn of the century. He died in 1901, shortly before the peace treaty he negotiated was signed.

Physiognomically, Li's face is a perfect example of the countenance of a leader destined to occupy high positions in government. His face is perfectly balanced and proportioned, except the chin, which forecast his less glamorous years as a minor provincial official.

This picture, taken when Clare Boothe Luce was named Ambassador to Italy in 1953, was chosen in preference to a more recent one because it shows clearly her hairline and forehead.

Her hairline is not clear-cut, which means a troubled childhood, a life that could be hectic into her early twenties, especially in marital matters. But her forehead, broad and full, indicates a high degree of intelligence and excellence in the literary field at an early age.

Her eyebrows (positions 31 through 34), which appear to be on a straight line but delicately separated, indicate not only her creative years but also her fighting spirit. And this is the period of her blissful marital life.

From the point of beauty, her eyes surpass her other features. They are controlled and possess glitter, indicating significant achievement ahead.

By the age of forty, which is reflected in the area between the two eyebrows and two eyes (positions 28 and 41), her fortune turns in a new direction—politics. Actually, she entered Congress in this period. These years are reflected in her nose bridge, which is straight, full, and forceful. Her fiftieth year, when she was named Ambassador to Italy, and the ensuing years are represented by her firm upper lip.

Her cheeklines are fine but not forceful (positions 56 and 57), signifying frustrations that eventually put an end to her political and diplomatic career.

She has a pointed chin, which does not match her other facial features. Since the chin governs the years from sixty-one to sixty-seven, many unfortunate things could happen to affect an otherwise happy life, such as a death in the family.

Taking her facial features as a whole, the physiognomist concludes that she will continue to use her literary talent to advantage and enjoy gracious living for many years to come.

MIN YONG-IK (1860–1914)

This is the photograph of a man of refined taste, intelligence, and geniality. He would have preferred to be a literary man or a poet rather than be called upon to assume the role of politician or diplomat. But fate dictated that he be chosen as the first Korean envoy to the United States at the age of twenty-three.

Despite his native Korean hat, his forehead is clearly shown to be broad and high, without sharp angles. This indicates high intelligence and foreshadows that the individual will occupy a high position in government.

The browbones are high and the eyebrows are very refined, indicating that he probably had two or three brothers. The areas between the two eyebrows (position 28) and between the two eyes (position 41) are full and solid. This confirms that he will hold high positions and win great honors. The eyes are fairly long and the irises well protected or "controlled." These are good signs and reflect a career of high achievement.

The years forty-one to fifty are the best of his life, a reading of his nose reveals. However, at position 51 the groove indicates that his good fortune will wane. The lips are weak and poor; the chin, the worst feature of all, recedes and is out of balance with the rest of the face; the beard is uncropped and scraggly.

Because of the weak chin, the upper lip is compromised, especially at the left corner of the mouth. Worse, the face lacks clear-cut cheeklines, without which the physiognomist can accurately predict death at fifty or shortly thereafter. In real life, Ambassador Min died at the age of fifty-four.

WILLIAM McKINLEY   (1843–1901)

This face is a rather uncomplicated one. The broad fore-head is formidable—high, full, and without any defect such as sharp slopes toward the temples on both sides. The area between the eyebrows (position 28) is full and significantly solid, without showing a hollow or weakened effect; this balances the forehead very well. Next, the area between the two eyes (position 41) is even more powerful than the area between the two eyebrows (position 28).

The contour of this face, oblong in shape, speaks amply that this is a man destined to occupy a high ruling position. The eyebrows bristling upward show him to be of brave and generous character. The cheekbones are high, meaning he will exercise extraordinary power. The nose is straight, high, and without defect of any kind, and its tip is well rounded and supported by well-shaped wings on both sides. The groove just below the nose tip is straight and uniform but shallow; this can be interpreted as indicating that he will have one or two children and will have a short lifespan. But the firm, broad upper lip should be read as years of greatness in terms of career.

The cheeklines (positions 56 and 57) are fine. However, the one on the right (position 57), though deep and broken, drops away too suddenly. The one to the left, which happens to be on the dark side, can still be detected as showing a bent line toward the mouth. This augurs ill.

In his fifty-eighth year, represented by the middle part of his right cheek (position 59), which is unfortunately blocked out by strong light, he will meet an unnatural death.

The expert face reader can predict McKinley's violent death for three reasons. First, his eyes, which are powerful but "uncontrolled," invite personal danger. Second, his cleft chin, so deep as to touch his chin bone, when considered in combination with his uncontrolled eyes confirms personal danger. Thirdly, his chin is ill-shaped on both sides and imbalanced in relation to the rest of his formidable face.

ELLEN SMITH   (–)

This is the picture of a criminal.

Her name was Ellen Smith, alias Evelyn Ellis, and she was the wife and then widow of the chief of a most daring band of criminals specializing in train robbery. Her part in these crimes was to scout the train stations and man the getaway car.

This picture was taken soon after her arrest in California in 1930. It shows her anger and defiance. And this makes reading her face much easier.

Her forehead indicates a sharp, resourceful degree of intelligence. But it is narrow on the front and sloped sharply to the temples on both sides, a sign of instability and a tendency to go to extremes without regard to consequences.

She had relatively no eyebrows, merely painted lines. Her eyes are her most revealing feature, exposed and uncontrolled. The left eye is "three-white-sided," and this, plus the oddly shaped eyelids, suggests the extraordinary spirit of a daredevil. When her two eyes are considered together, they foretell disaster.

Her nose bridge appears long and straight, but if examined carefully it is actually "irregular." This covers the period from forty-one to fifty in her life, the years of greatest personal dangers.

Her lips show lewdness. The lower lip is that of a libertine. Her jawbones are set widely apart and protrude backward. This points to unreliability and an untrustworthy character, a willingness and readiness to betray a friend.

To the face reader this is decidedly the countenance of a criminal. Although judging by her broad forehead this woman came from a good and respectable family, she was endowed with an unmanageable disposition and temperament. She was born to defy the law.

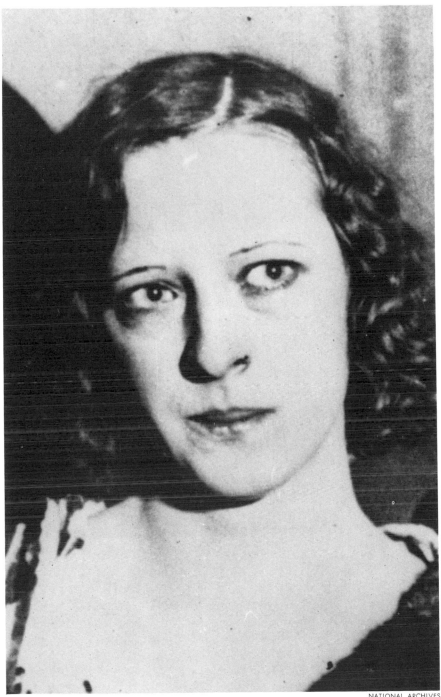

JAMES FORRESTAL   (1892–1949)

James Forrestal was a man of great talent and unbending determination. This aspect of his character can readily be seen from his powerful forehead, which is broad, high, and well balanced.

His first success began at the age of thirty-one, as indicated by the outer side of his left eyebrow, which is set on a high browbone. By thirty-four he became the vice-president of a prestigious bank and then rose to its presidency at the age of forty-six. The success was reflected in powerful eyes, nose bridge, and cheekbones.

Further fast promotions can be seen in his powerful upper lip (positions 52 through 55), the period corresponding to his appointments first as Secretary of the Navy and then Secretary of Defense.

Overall, his face suggests a man suffering inwardly the unbearable pain of frustration because his impatience got the better of him. This is revealed in the area between the two eyebrows and the two eyes.

His cheeklines (positions 56 and 57) are neither deep nor clear-cut. Even so, without these lines his success would have been cut short in these years. Examined closely, we find the right line unclear and weak; on the left the line is broken, an ominous sign. The chin and jawbones are unusually weak and do not balance the forehead and eyes. The contrast is obvious—indeed, extreme.

A physiognomist concludes that this is a "topheavy" face, ill-balanced, the face of an individual with a short lifespan. The most critical years, as reflected in the cheekline, would be fifty-six or fifty-seven.

He committed suicide at fifty-seven.

ADOLF HITLER (1889–1945)

To a physiognomist, in this face all the characteristics of evil are brought into the open.

The facial skin is too tight for a normal person, which suggests a ruthless character. The eyes reflect unrelenting cruelty. The forehead is low between the eyebrows and hairline but unusually broad, which indicates intrepidity and intelligence. The small square areas between the eyebrows and the eyes are firm and raised, indicating an iron will. The high nose bridge, well balanced by high cheekbones, indicate a destiny of unlimited power.

His eyebrows (positions 31 through 34), pinpoint his rise to power in Germany as leader of the National Socialist German Workers' Party. His coarse eyebrows indicate contempt for the law and, interestingly, in this period he landed in prison. Beneath his eyes, on both sides, a hollow effect through which a line is visibly flowing downward across the cheek suggests Satanism. In Hitler's case it meant unparalleled disaster for the world and for himself.

His groove, representing age fifty (position 51), is invisible because of his thick, coarse mustache. However, to the expert, his upper lip is firm, and this marks his years of triumph, from fifty-one to fifty-six.

Hitler had no cheeklines to speak of. Without a pronounced cheekline on either side to balance his otherwise powerful features, disaster or personal danger was bound to result at or after age fifty-six. In Hitler's case, his cheeklines were barely a fraction of an inch long, and this presaged his downfall. Furthermore, his jawbones and chin were shapeless, out of balance with the powerful features above the nose. His defeat and death can be seen in these factors.

GEORGE C. MARSHALL   (1880–1959)

To the physiognomist, this is the face of a man of great organizing talent, an individual who is meticulous with detail. This is shown by the broad forehead with gentle slopes on both sides toward the temples. In a way, the forehead is slightly unbalanced relative to the other facial features, indicating a reserved nature, a loner who prefers to work out his problems and plans by himself. This is also the face of a methodical, cautious individual, as shown by the two horizontal forehead lines.

The eyebrows are lower than the ears, indicating intelligence and logical thinking. Both of the eyes slant slightly downward at the outer corners, but the irises are fully controlled. Position 41 is weak, however, and this and the eyebrows and eyes indicate obscurity between the years thirty and forty. However, at the age of forty-one his talents were first recognized. The nose is literally a clue to a career of increasing importance and high honor. Although the groove is weak, the upper lip is firm and full, suggesting great responsibility in government.

The jawbones and chin are those of a planner. In fact, the jawbones are not strong enough to balance a powerful forehead, which indicates he will not achieve the highest position in government.

The face is stern but at heart these are the features of the man of goodwill. This is also the countenance of a person with a reasonable nature but whose mind is set once he comes to a decision. This characteristic is also shown in the eyes, which are controlled and decisive.

Although the chin is of the protruding type, it is not broad enough to balance the forehead. This indicates that his rise to power will be measured. Finally, the chin suggests longevity, death at the age of seventy-nine or later.

MADAME CHIANG KAI-SHEK   (1898–   )

This semiprofile photo, taken some years ago, strikingly reveals Madame Chiang's character, station of life, and achievements. The physiognomist's first impression is that she has superior intelligence and soaring ambition. She is destined to occupy positions of power and is endowed with a long life accompanied by luxury and high honors. The sharp angles shown in this photo are pregnant with meaning, the most pronounced of which indicates that Madame Chiang is an unusually strong-willed personality.

Her top hairline is relatively narrow, signifying her family origins, that is, before age fifteen: modest, perhaps slightly better than average. The forehead, from the hairline down to the middle point between the eyebrows, is high, wide, and full, and in these years (positions 15 through 28) her educational and social foundations were prepared for a rapid rise to prominence. Horizontally (positions 29 and 30), she should achieve sudden fame.

Her browbones are high and elegant, and the brows are refined (positions 31 through 34)—the years of positions of power. Her features also show a high degree of artistic and creative talents.

Madame Chiang's eyes, with flashing "glitter," are well positioned, well balanced, and well controlled. However, there is a flaw—her eyes are a little too small to balance the structure of her face. The flaw is not important enough to jeopardize her personal fortune, but it does detract from her position of power.

Her cheekbones are unusually high and sharp, indicating not only a woman of strong will but also one beset with marital problems. But these cheekbones, high and sharp,

compensate the flaw in the eyes. In her case, there is the saving grace of her intelligence and a resigned realization that tolerance, not necessarily submission, is the key to a peaceful life with her domineering husband, the Generalissimo.

Her nose is straight and faultless (positions 41 through 50), and these are the years she should head important national organizations. The groove (position 51) is not pronounced, meaning childlessness. The chin is upturned enough to balance her forehead, a very important factor reflecting the fortunes of her later life.

Weighing all the above values, the analysis indicates that her life is decidedly one of high honors, power, and luxury. After sixty-five she tends to withdraw from public activities. But she will continue to sponsor worthy causes and hold the limelight throughout old age.

DR. MARTIN LUTHER KING, JR.

(1929–1968)

Since Dr. King has gone down in history as a spiritual leader in the struggle for civil rights, like Gandhi of India, several of his facial features should suggest that he is a man of extraordinary character. His face should also provide a clue to his death at the hands of an assassin.

To the physiognomist, King's face is decidedly that of a martyr. His massive forehead dominates, even destroys, the values of his other features. This reveals that his lifetime work is crowded into a short span of less than fourteen years, that is, from the age of twenty-six to the years represented by the eyes (positions 35 through 40). His face is extremely unusual, suggesting the interplay of great fame and great danger. This is the more so because no feature below his forehead and eyes is strong enough to balance his other features.

First, let's measure his three zones. The First Zone, from the top hairline to the middle point between the two brows, is far longer than either of the other two zones. This indicates that any great achievement in his life must be achieved before age forty. His forehead is unusually high and full. The corridor (positions 15, 16, 19, 22, 25, and 28) is somewhat raised, judging by the highlight on both corners in this photo, indicating the most active years of his life. The highlighted areas (positions 17, 18, 20, 21, 23, 24, 26, and 27) are equally full and solid and indicate continuously active years.

Beneath the brows are prominent browbones that are so high they show fame as well as spiritual leadership, from the age of twenty-five or twenty-six (positions 26 and 27) onwards. On both sides of the forehead (positions 20, 21,

WIDE WORLD PHOTOS

23, 24, 26, 27, 29, and 30) there are sudden drops or slopes that suggest entanglement with the law. They also forewarn of personal danger.

His brows (positions 31 through 34) are powerful but unfortunately on either side they fall off. This represents the years of head-on conflict with the law. But, it must be noted, these are also the years when he may achieve the most for his movement.

Dr. King's eyes (positions 35 through 40) represent ages thirty-four to thirty-nine, and these are the most turbulent and dangerous years in his life. On the one hand, there is powerful glitter in both pupils—the world will shower on him great honors, awards, and fame. On the other, these are the most dangerous years as reflected by what is called the "three-white-sided" eye, which portends violence to a person.

Other features below the eyes are also unfortunately out of balance. The nose is too flat and weak. The cheekbones slant downward. The cheeklines are short and indistinct. The groove is flat and too wide. The chin is especially weak, indicating a difficult and frustrated childhood and a short life. Taken together, none of these features is well balanced or well proportioned, and the physiognomist cannot read beyond the years thirty-nine to forty.

Dr. King was a dreamer but also an activist. He was a man of high resolve, and once his principles were laid down he would challenge whatever obstacles stood in his way. He was kindhearted, trustworthy, and an affectionate family man. His cruel fate overtook him in the prime of life.

DWIGHT D. EISENHOWER   (1890–1969)

This face is a perfect delight for the physiognomist because it is in perfect balance and proportion. It is oblong in shape. The head is powerful. The eyebrows are set on high browbones. The eyes are perfectly matched and controlled. The cheekbones on both sides of the eyes are strongly marked. These are the portents of a ruler.

The area between the eyebrows (position 28) is slightly less full than the area between the eyes (position 41). The nose bridge, powerfully formed, is straight, high, and even, and the nose tip is well supported by two well-matched wings. The lips are firm and full, and the mouth is long and evenly shaped. In these circumstances, the physiognomist's first impression is that this is the face of destiny, the man who will rise to be a commander and ruler of people.

Undoubtedly, the best features are the lips, mouth, and chin. As a composite they are in good balance and proportion.

In practical terms, the face indicates that the individual's greatest years will be from fifty-one to sixty-six. Actually, this covers the span during which Eisenhower was President, after a rapid rise from brigadier general.

The chin, representing the years sixty to seventy-one, is superb in form and strength. During this period, of course, he was twice elected President.

Despite a brilliant record, however, the face is not entirely free of defect. The cheeklines, for example, are comparatively weak. The left one is somewhat broken, and the right, in the shade, though faintly visible, is also weak. These govern the years fifty-five and fifty-six and indicate the beginning of poor health, frustration, and even a change of career. The groove under the nose tip is straight, but it is also short and shallow, meaning this individual will probably not live beyond eighty years.

The mouth, at the two ends, is also overextended, a further indication of poor health and slow deterioration, especially at age sixty-five (note that position 66 is seemingly compromised below by a bent chin line.)

Apart from these defects, the physiognomist would also note that the ears, which are adequate, have no long or solid lobes. Moreover, the chin is insufficiently full. These signs also point to poor health very late in life.

At his death, Eisenhower was seventy-nine.

A JAPANESE WARRIOR   (–)

This photograph provides insight into the face of a professional soldier, in this case a member of the Samurai, the Japanese warrior class, a man who pledged his honor and life to his clan. This is the face of a fearless and courageous individual, always prepared to accept a challenge on the field of battle or to challenge others at the slightest provocation.

The forehead is relatively narrow and ill-balanced, typical of the zealot. In the case of the Samurari warrior, he was prepared to commit suicide (hara-kiri) to vindicate his honor, whether the need was real or fanciful.

Physiognomically, the browbones are high and hence the eyebrows are also set high. This means the individual should occupy a high position in society. The eyes are fairly long, even longer than necessary to balance the face. This indicates a high position of considerable authority. However, the eyeballs protrude and the left iris is off-center, a sign of unbalance. These negative features suggest personal danger. Since both eyes are uncontrolled, this points to an unstable, explosive character.

But the individual's nose bridge is straight, solid, and long, indicating that he may achieve fame between the ages of forty and fifty. After fifty it is difficult to judge his destiny. The cheeklines (positions 56 and 57) are obscure; the upper lip is thin; the chin recedes; and the jawbones are narrow. These defects are not balanced by the nose. The face reader, accordingly, would conclude that after age fifty this warrior would either meet a violent death or simply fade away.

Although social conditions in feudal Japan of the last century and in contemporary America are worlds apart, daredevils and professional criminals in today's culture may be observed to share similar facial characteristics with this photograph.

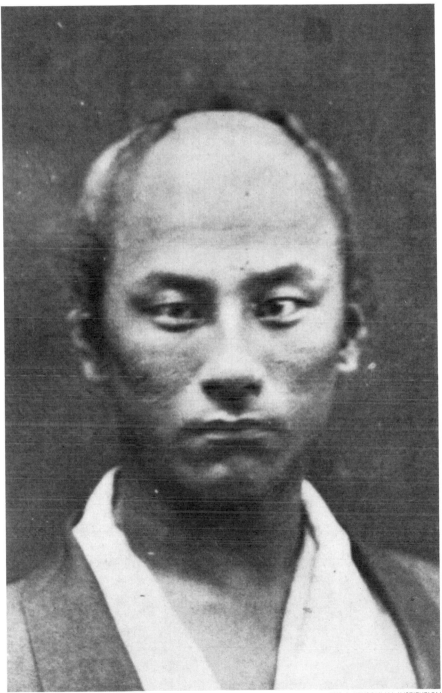

FRANZ KAFKA   (1883–1924)

Kafka's face is obviously of the "irregular" type, ill-balanced and out of proportion. Yet he managed through creative work to attain universal acclaim as a novelist—significantly only after his death.

Kafka's is a very sad face. Sad because he was born to a tyrannically patriarchal family and was never permitted the opportunity to develop his ideas. This is clearly reflected in his top hairline, which is jagged, low-lying, and extends across the forehead in an even curving line from one ear to another. Such a hairline is quite unusual. A normal person's hairline invariably has a break or angle somewhere near or above the temple on both sides. Kafka's hairline unmistakably indicates that he had a wretched and neurotic childhood. He was trapped in a deepening sense of guilt from which he never seemed able to free himself.

However, Kafka had a broad forehead set against a triangular face, evidence of high, innate intelligence. This too is shown in his browbones, which are also high. His eyebrows (positions 31 through 34) are powerful. These features point to literary genius. These were also the years when he dreamed, in straitened circumstances, of things mystical and interpreted them in the artistic expression of weird emotions rarely possessed by other writers.

But his brows overpower his eyes, and this spells tragedy. Admittedly, his eyes (positions 35 through 40) are fairly large and animated, and therefore actually represent his productive years in literary pursuits. However, these eyes are "exposed," "uncontrolled," "glitterless," and "death-darting." This marks a period of tragic bouts with sickness, broken romances, and chronic mental depression. Ironi-

cally, these strains sharpened his wits, deepened his insight, and enhanced his creative literary power.

But the most critical years are yet to come, as indicated near the "roots" of the nose, involving three positions: position 41, the middle point between the two eyes; position 42, the left side near the inner end of the left eye; and position 43, the right side opposite position 42. These are the critical years because they are affected by weakened eyes and by an ominous line known as the "Suspending Needle" (positions 28 and 41), which in combination with the eyes heightened his tragic destiny.

Position 42 is near the left eye, which is weaker than the right, being hollow and ill-balanced. It is here that the physiognomist pinpoints the terminal year.

Admittedly, because Kafka's face is of the "irregular" type, the values of each facial feature must be analyzed entirely on the basis of balance and proportion. If we examine his nose, which is fairly straight, and his mouth, which is seemingly broad, we still find them out of balance with his forehead.

Kafka's tragedy ended when he died at forty-one.

ANDY WARHOL   (1927–   )

Here's a dynamic face—that of a creative writer, musician, or artist. Dynamic because it reflects talent, vitality,
and the courage to be independent by creating a world of
its own. Andy Warhol, convinced of his art, worked hard
with an inflexible determination to win universal recognition.

In physiognomical parlance, his face is "irregular," for
most of the features cannot be gauged by rule of thumb as
is the case in the great majority of people. This is because
vital features are off balance or out of proportion. But
when viewed as a whole, there is a semblance of unity in
this face, and this makes him an extraordinary man.

His forehead (though mostly covered by hair in the
present photo) is very wide and full, and especially the left
high point. Assuming the right high point is identical, this
shows superior intelligence and organizing power. But it
must be noted that being the creative type, he has no use
for traditionally accepted standards. As indicated by his
ears and relatively low forehead, he was not born to a rich
or even a comfortable family, and this accounts for an early
life of arduous, sustained struggle. His is the face of a self-
made man, a pioneer in thought and action.

His browbones are high, signifying success and fame at
an early age, before thirty. His brows are powerful
(though the left one is obscured by the highlight in this
photo) and in fact too powerful for his eyes.

Of all his features, his eyes are something of a paradox
(positions 35 through 40). They represent at once strength
and weakness. By strength, the physiognomist means great
successes; by weakness is meant danger to his person. In the

CONSTANTIN/VOGELMANN

first place, his eyes are not identical, as the right contains far more penetrating "glitter" than the left. And the left eye is smaller than the right. Finally, the pupils are out of balance, indicating perpetual conflict. These are the signs of personal danger in life, especially between the ages of thirty-six and thirty-eight (not later than forty-one). But these are also the years his dreams will come to fruition and he is likely to achieve fame. In point of success, these years are extremely important for having laid solid foundations for a great future.

Warhol's nose is straight, full, and solid (positions 41 through 50). These are the years when he finds full expression for his art. His groove (position 51) is clear-cut and good. His upper lip (positions 52 through 55) is firm, though both of the outer ends are slightly uneven. This also points to successful years. His cheeklines (positions 56 and 57) are neither deep nor clear. Also, the side cheeklines (positions 58 and 59) are unusual and should be interpreted as a period of tremendous effort accompanied by minor successes and personal danger. His mouth and chin are broad and firm; they balance well with other features. This suggests comparatively better years.

Taking his facial features as a whole, the conclusion is that this is the face of a very gifted artist, a dreamer and a performer. Yet he appears passive, much the way a free, unfettered Taoist mind works, and herein lies his real power. Thus he is soft-spoken and loath to satiate his ego. He is a leader and an organizer, the secret of his success and fame.

Warhol is innovative. He has the courage of his convictions. He is a trailblazer. But he is prone to danger.

ROBERT S. McNAMARA (1916–)

Judging by the contour of his face, some remarkable features can be easily seen. First, he has a powerful forehead —broad, high, full—matched by well-controlled eyes and an almost perfect nose. This is decidedly a superior face, the countenance of a fortunate man who is able, energetic, and intelligent.

McNamara has had a happy childhood and matured early. His adult life was satisfactory because of rapid promotions and successes. His face shows that he is destined to be highly placed in any organization with which he chooses to associate himself. Such a face will succeed not by luck but by sheer ability and astuteness, because he approaches his problems with coolness and discharges his duties methodically and efficiently.

Intellectually, he could be a scholar, but the pace would be too slow for his temperament. He feels at home in the active world, wrestling with tough challenges.

The most striking features are his eyes, which are truly "controlled" and perfectly balanced with powerful "glitter." The eyes alone spell success and achievement, for, according to the old Chinese texts, they reflect a person's inner energy, which in turn reflects his intuitive mind and positive actions.

McNamara's formal career begins at about the age of thirty (position 31), as reflected in the outer end of the left eyebrow. Both of his eyebrows are refined, the type that seems to prepare the way for greater things to come. So his promotions in these years were steady and sure. At ages thirty-four to thirty-nine, governed by his brilliant eyes

(positions 35 through 40), he reaches the higher echelons of command.

Physiognomically, his nose bridge is formidable (positions 41 through 45, that is, ages forty to forty-four). It is high, straight, full, imposing, and flawless, signifying phenomenal promotions to higher and more responsible positions. In fact, at this period of his life he moved from the presidency of the Ford Motor Company to the Kennedy Cabinet as Secretary of Defense.

His groove, lips, cheeklines and cheeks governing the years between fifty and fifty-eight (positions 51 through 59) are solid, clear-cut, and well formed, presaging a continuation in high positions of power. Circumstances may cause him to change positions, but this would hardly lessen his powers, lower his rank or impair his prestige.

At this writing, he is the president of the World Bank, and he is likely to remain at that post for a while. If we further examine his chin, jawbones, cheekbones and ears, we will find that they all contribute to the balance and proportion of his facial features as a whole. For these reasons, there are greater things in store for him, either returning to the government or heading a giant industry.

HENRY A. KISSINGER   (1923–   )

The most striking thing about Kissinger's face is that it is just about perfectly proportioned. Note the three zones, which seem to be mathematically divided in equal length, that is, (1) from the top hairline to the middle of the eyebrows; (2) from the eyebrows to the nose tip; and (3) from the nose tip to the tip of the chin. To the physiognomist, it is an axiomatic truth that the better the proportion and balance, the better the augury for a continuously brilliant and distinguished career.

Kissinger's face is of the semitriangular type, which, in his case, means a combination of the triangular and the oblong. In physiognomical terms, he is basically an intellectual and in time destined to become a highly placed government or institutional official. The shape of his face marks him a superb strategist, wielding tremendous influence, articulate and able to act with authority.

In fact, this type of face can be easily recognized as that of an extraordinary person because it is balanced and well proportioned, with practically no serious defects. And in his case, there seems a salutary effect that a small defect can be compensated by the combined perfect structure of other features.

His ears, though much obscured in this photo, are relatively short for his face, but they should not be interpreted as a serious defect, perhaps during old age only. As such, they reflect simply an unhappy childhood.

By the ages of fourteen to fifteen (positions 15 and 16), the beginning of his adulthood, his lifestyle takes on a new turn, and for the better. This change in fortune is reflected in his forehead, one of the most important facial features.

Kissinger's forehead is formidable because of its width, length, and contour, all of which seem perfectly proportioned. The vertical corridor in the central area—from the

U.S. DEPARTMENT OF STATE

hairline to the middle point between the two eyebrows (positions 15, 16, 19, 22, 25, and 28)—is full and stream-lined. Intersecting with this corridor are three or four horizontal lines, deep and clear, as in harmonic formation. These are interpreted as signs of fame and greatness either as a thinker, writer, or high government official.

From the ages of twenty-eight and twenty-nine he is already a well-seasoned thinker and planner, in a position to counsel those in power. The years thirty to thirty-three (positions 31 through 34) are reflected in his eyebrows, which are long and refined, indicating a crescendo of fame and successes. And these are the years when solid foundations are laid to prepare himself for the greater things to come.

But the most formidable feature on his face is his nose (positions 41 through 50), which is straight, full, and supported on both sides by ideally shaped nostril wings. His nose tip is of rare perfection (position 48). These features signify auspicious years should he find himself in the right position to realize his ideas and dreams.

The years forty-four through fifty should be the happiest, when he reaches the pinnacle of power. Indeed, since 1969 he has been the architect of President Nixon's foreign policy. At this writing, at age fifty (position 51), he is Secretary of State. His upper lip is unusually firm (positions 52 through 55), signifying that he will continue to enjoy unmatched fame and success regardless of changes in official title or position. However, his cheeklines (positions 56 and 57) are imperfect, especially on the right, as shown in this photo. It is short and unpronounced. The left line runs downward tenuously in a sort of broken fashion. These features foreshadow a period of decline, probably withdrawal from the limelight. It would be to his interest to watch his health.

However, his chin is broad enough to compensate other imperfections, if not to balance his formidable nose. His chin has a deep-cut line (position 62), according to this photo, signifying reverses. In any case, this later period will consist of quiet years, if health permits, and his intellectual prowess will remain undiminished.

CHAPTER 18

NOW ANALYZE YOURSELF!

AGAINST the background of the preceding chapters, it is time to examine and analyze your own face and thereby test your face-reading ability. Now you can readily apply the rules developed by Chinese physiognomists over the centuries.

Bear in mind that the system is integrated. That is, it must be viewed as a whole. It is pointless to study a few highlights in this book and then try to render an intelligent reading. The whole face, each of the Five Vital Features, plus all other aspects must be considered together with balance and proportion. Your reading must reflect a sense of facial unity.

There are those who will read carefully through these pages and still not be able to effectively apply the principles set forth. In such a case, very often all that is needed is self-confidence. Continual practice is imperative, on yourself, on relatives and friends, on associates and others.

From studying living case histories you can enrich your own face-reading techniques and abilities. For regular training, merely study the photographs in your daily newspaper or glance across the aisle and study the faces of the strangers opposite you in a bus, subway, or train. You will surprise yourself with your growing knowledge and ability to judge personality and destiny on the basis of face reading.

As the Chinese say, "Hao yun ch'i"—good luck!